Norwegian fjord Cruise

Travel Guide

Discover Stunning Waterfalls, Glaciers, and Picturesque Villages Along Norway's Coast.

2025

Bobby L. Sanders

Table of Contents

Chapter 1. Welcome to the Norwegian Fjords

Welcome to the Norwegian Fjords

Nestled between towering cliffs and cascading waterfalls, the Norwegian fjords are a breathtaking spectacle of nature's artistry. This region, known for its deep, narrow inlets carved by glaciers, offers a journey into some of the world's most awe-inspiring landscapes. Whether you're an adventurer, a nature lover, or someone seeking tranquility, the fjords welcome you with open arms. Here's a glimpse into the magic that awaits you in the Norwegian fjords.

The fjords are a geological marvel, with steep mountains plunging into deep blue waters, creating dramatic vistas at every turn. The sheer cliffs, dotted with lush greenery and cascading waterfalls, form a stunning contrast against the tranquil fjord waters. Each fjord has its unique charm, from the UNESCO World Heritage-listed Geirangerfjord, known for its "Seven Sisters" waterfall, to the tranquil Nærøyfjord, one of the narrowest fjords in the world.

1. Spectacular Scenery

2. Outdoor Adventures

For those with an adventurous spirit, the fjords offer a plethora of activities. Hiking trails, such as the famous Pulpit Rock and Trolltunga, provide panoramic views that will take your breath away. Kayaking on the fjord waters lets you explore hidden coves and remote beaches, while glacier hiking and ice climbing offer thrilling experiences on ancient ice formations. Each adventure promises a deep connection with nature and unforgettable memories.

3. Rich Cultural Heritage

The Norwegian fjords are not just about natural beauty; they are also steeped in rich cultural heritage. The charming villages along the fjords, like Flåm and Aurland, offer a glimpse into traditional Norwegian life. Explore historic stave churches, visit local museums, and immerse yourself in the folklore and traditions that have shaped this region. The fjords have been home to fishermen, farmers, and traders for centuries, and their stories are woven into the fabric of the landscape.

4. Wildlife and Marine Life

The fjords are teeming with wildlife, both on land and in the water. Look out for majestic sea eagles soaring above, and keep an eye on the waters for seals and porpoises. The fjords are also a prime spot for whale watching, with orcas and humpback whales often making appearances. Bird watchers will be delighted by the variety of seabirds, including puffins and kittiwakes, that nest along the cliffs.

5. Culinary Delights

Norwegian cuisine, with its emphasis on fresh, locally sourced ingredients, is a treat for the senses. Indulge in fresh seafood, such as salmon and cod, or try traditional dishes like rakfisk (fermented fish) and klippfisk (dried cod). Don't miss the chance to taste local cheeses, cured meats, and freshly baked bread. Pair your meal with a glass of aquavit, a traditional Scandinavian spirit, for an authentic culinary experience.

6. Sustainable Travel

Norway is a leader in sustainable travel, and the fjord region is no exception. Many tour operators and accommodations are committed to eco-friendly practices, ensuring that the natural beauty of the fjords is preserved for future generations. From electric ferries to sustainable hiking trails, you can enjoy your visit knowing that you're minimizing your environmental footprint.

The Norwegian fjords are a destination like no other, offering a harmonious blend of natural beauty, outdoor adventure, cultural heritage, and culinary delights. Whether you're gazing at the fjords' dramatic landscapes, embarking on thrilling activities, or savoring local flavors, each moment in the fjords is a celebration of the extraordinary. Welcome to the Norwegian fjords—where every journey is an exploration of wonder and every vista is a masterpiece of nature.

I hope this guide inspires you to explore the magic of the Norwegian fjords. Enjoy your adventure, my friends!

Brief History of the Norwegian Fjords

The Norwegian fjords are renowned for their breathtaking beauty, dramatic landscapes, and rich history. These natural wonders were formed over millions of years through a combination of geological processes and glacial activity. The history of the Norwegian fjords is a fascinating tale that encompasses the forces of nature, ancient civilizations, and cultural evolution. Let's delve into the extensive history of these magnificent fjords.

1. Geological Formation

Glacial Origins:
• The formation of the Norwegian fjords dates back to the last Ice Age, around 2.6 million years ago. During this period, massive glaciers covered much of Norway, extending far into the sea. As the glaciers advanced and retreated over millennia, they carved deep, narrow valleys into the landscape, creating the fjords we see today.

U-shaped Valleys:
• The glacial activity resulted in the characteristic U-shaped valleys of the fjords. The immense weight and movement of the glaciers eroded the rock, deepening and widening the valleys. As the ice melted and receded, seawater flooded the valleys, forming the fjords.

Mountainous Surroundings:
• The steep, towering cliffs that surround the fjords are a result of the glacial erosion and tectonic activity. The combination of these geological processes created the dramatic and rugged landscapes that define the Norwegian fjords.

2. Early Human Inhabitants

Stone Age Settlements:
• The first human inhabitants of the fjord region arrived during the Stone Age, around 10,000 years ago. These early settlers were hunter-gatherers who relied on the abundant natural resources of the fjords, including fish, game, and plant materials.

Archaeological Discoveries:
• Archaeological evidence, such as stone tools, cave paintings, and burial mounds, provides insights into the lives of these early inhabitants. Sites like the Rock Carvings of Alta, a UNESCO World Heritage site, showcase intricate carvings depicting scenes of hunting, fishing, and daily life.

Bronze Age and Iron Age:
• During the Bronze Age (around 1800-500 BCE) and the Iron Age (around 500 BCE-800 CE), the fjord region saw the development of more advanced societies. People began to engage in agriculture, trade, and metalworking. The discovery of bronze and iron tools, as well as burial mounds, indicates a shift towards more complex social structures.

3. Viking Era

Viking Expansion:
• The Viking Age (around 800-1050 CE) was a significant period in the history of the Norwegian fjords. The fjords provided natural harbors and safe havens for the Viking

longships, making them ideal bases for exploration, trade, and raiding.

Maritime Prowess:
• The Vikings were master shipbuilders and navigators. Their longships, designed for speed and maneuverability, allowed them to traverse the fjords and venture far beyond Norway's shores. The fjords were crucial to their maritime success, offering access to the open sea and sheltered anchorages.

Settlements and Trade:
• During the Viking Age, settlements and trading posts flourished along the fjords. Towns like Bergen and Stavanger became important centers of commerce and culture. The Vikings established trade routes that connected Norway to the British Isles, Europe, and beyond.

Cultural Legacy:
• The Viking legacy is still evident in the fjord region today. Museums, archaeological sites, and festivals celebrate the rich cultural heritage of the Vikings. The Viking Ship Museum in Oslo, for example, houses well-preserved Viking ships and artifacts that provide a glimpse into the lives of these seafaring warriors.

4. Medieval and Early Modern Period

Christianization and Kingdom Formation:
• The medieval period saw the Christianization of Norway and the establishment of the Norwegian kingdom. The fjords played a vital role in the spread of Christianity, with churches and monasteries being built along their shores. Stave churches, such as the Urnes Stave Church, are architectural masterpieces from this era.

Hanseatic League:
• In the late medieval period, the Hanseatic League, a powerful trading alliance of German merchant cities, established a significant presence in Bergen. The Hanseatic merchants dominated trade in the region, exporting fish and other goods from the fjords to Europe.

Agricultural and Fishing Communities:
• Throughout the early modern period, the fjords were home to thriving agricultural and fishing communities. The fertile lands and abundant marine resources sustained these communities, and traditional practices such as fishing, farming, and livestock raising continued to shape their way of life.

5. Modern Era and Tourism

Industrialization and Development:
• The 19th and 20th centuries brought industrialization and modernization to the fjord region. The development of infrastructure, such as roads, railways, and ports, facilitated trade and transportation. Industries like shipbuilding, fishing, and energy production became important economic drivers.

Tourism Boom:
• The natural beauty of the fjords began to attract tourists in the late 19th century. Artists, writers, and explorers, captivated by the stunning landscapes, helped promote the fjords as a travel destination. Today, tourism is a major industry, with visitors from around the

world coming to experience the fjords' breathtaking scenery and outdoor activities.

Sustainable Practices:

• In recent years, there has been a growing focus on sustainability and environmental conservation in the fjord region. Efforts to protect the natural environment, promote eco-friendly tourism, and preserve cultural heritage are vital to ensuring the fjords' long-term health and appeal.

The history of the Norwegian fjords is a rich tapestry woven from geological processes, human ingenuity, and cultural evolution. From their formation during the last Ice Age to their significance during the Viking Era and their status as a modern tourism destination, the fjords have played a central role in shaping Norway's identity. Exploring the history of the fjords offers a deeper appreciation of their beauty, resilience, and enduring legacy.

Chapter 2. Planning Your Norwegian Fjord Cruise

Best Time to Visit

The Norwegian fjords are a breathtaking destination that offers stunning landscapes, unique experiences, and unforgettable memories. The best time to visit the Norwegian fjords largely depends on what you want to see and do. Here's a detailed guide to help you decide the perfect time for your adventure:

- **Spring (April to May)**

Why Visit:
• **Milder Weather**: Spring brings milder temperatures, with daytime highs ranging from 8°C to 15°C (46°F to 59°F). The days start to get longer, and the snow begins to melt, revealing lush greenery and blooming flowers.
• **Waterfalls in Full Flow**: As the snow melts, the waterfalls are at their most powerful, creating a spectacular sight as they cascade down the fjord cliffs.
• Fewer Crowds: Spring is considered the shoulder season, so you can enjoy the beauty of the fjords without the summer crowds.

Visiting the fjords in spring is a magical experience. The landscape awakens from its winter slumber, and the air is filled with the scent of fresh blooms. The sight of roaring waterfalls against the backdrop of vibrant greenery is simply mesmerizing. It's the perfect time for peaceful hikes and scenic drives.

- ### Summer (June to August)

Why Visit:
- **Warmest Weather**: Summer offers the warmest weather, with daytime highs ranging from 15°C to 25°C (59°F to 77°F). The long days and the Midnight Sun phenomenon allow for extended exploration and outdoor activities.
- **Best for Outdoor Activities**: Summer is ideal for hiking, kayaking, and boat tours. The fjord waters are calm, and the weather is perfect for outdoor adventures.
- **Lively Festivals and Events**: Summer is the season for local festivals and cultural events, providing an opportunity to experience Norwegian traditions and cuisine.

Summer in the fjords is a time of endless daylight and boundless energy. I spent my days hiking along scenic trails, kayaking in crystal-clear waters, and exploring charming villages. The long, warm evenings were perfect for enjoying outdoor concerts and local festivals. The vibrant atmosphere and stunning landscapes made every moment unforgettable.

- ### Autumn (September to October)

Why Visit:
- **Stunning Autumn Colors**: The fjords are painted in shades of red, orange, and gold as the foliage changes color, creating a picturesque landscape.

- **Crisp, Clear Air**: The weather is still mild, with daytime highs ranging from 10°C to 18°C (50°F to 64°F). The crisp, clear air enhances the visibility of the stunning vistas.
- **Northern Lights**: As autumn progresses, there's a chance to witness the mesmerizing Northern Lights in the night sky.

Autumn in the fjords is a feast for the senses. The vivid colors of the foliage, the crispness of the air, and the serenity of the landscape create a magical atmosphere. I loved taking leisurely hikes through the vibrant forests and enjoying the tranquility of the fjords. The highlight of my trip was catching a glimpse of the Northern Lights dancing across the sky.

- ### Winter (November to March)

Why Visit:
- **Snow-Capped Beauty**: Winter transforms the fjords into a snowy wonderland, with snow-capped mountains and frozen waterfalls creating a serene and magical landscape.
- **Winter Sports**: Winter is perfect for skiing, snowboarding, and snowshoeing. Many fjord regions have excellent ski resorts and winter activities.
- **Northern Lights**: Winter is the best time to see the Northern Lights, with long nights providing ample opportunities to witness this natural phenomenon.

Winter in the fjords is like stepping into a fairy tale. The snow-covered landscape and the quiet serenity create a peaceful and otherworldly atmosphere. I enjoyed skiing down pristine slopes, exploring charming villages adorned with holiday lights, and cozying up by the fire in a rustic cabin. The highlight of my trip was witnessing the Northern Lights illuminate the night sky in a spectacular display.

The best time to visit the Norwegian fjords depends on your preferences and interests. Whether you choose the vibrant energy of summer, the tranquil beauty of spring and autumn, or the serene magic of winter, the fjords offer an unforgettable experience in every season. Each time of year brings its own unique charm and opportunities for adventure and discovery

Travel Documents and Requirements

To travel to Norway, you'll need to ensure you have the following documents and meet the necessary requirements:

Passport Requirements
• Validity: Your passport must be valid for at least three months beyond your planned departure from the Schengen area.
• Date of Issue: Your passport must have been issued within the last 10 years.
• Blank Pages: Ensure your passport has at least two blank pages for entry and exit stamps.

Visa Requirements
• Visa-Free Travel: If you're a citizen of a Schengen area country, you can travel to Norway without a visa for up to 90 days within a 180-day period.
• Visa for Longer Stays: If you plan to stay longer than 90 days, you'll need to apply for a

visa or residence permit. Check with the Norwegian Embassy for specific requirements.

Travel Insurance
• **Medical Coverage**: You must have travel medical insurance with a minimum coverage of €30,000 for the duration of your stay in the Schengen area.

Accommodation Proof
• **Hotel Booking**: You may need to show proof of your accommodation, such as a hotel booking confirmation or proof of address if you're staying with friends or family.

Financial Proof
• **Sufficient Funds**: You'll need to prove that you have enough money to cover your stay in Norway. The required amount varies depending on your accommodation and length of stay.

Return Ticket
• **Roundtrip Ticket**: You must have a confirmed roundtrip ticket with fixed travel dates.

Additional Documents
• **Travel Itinerary**: If you're traveling independently, you may need to provide a detailed travel plan or schedule.
• **Employment or Study Documents**: If applicable, provide documents related to your employment, school, or studies, along with permission for leave if needed.

For Minors
• **Consent Letter**: If you're traveling alone or with one parent, you'll need a letter of consent signed by both parents. If the parent you're

traveling with has sole custody, provide a certificate of single custody.

Health and Safety
• **Vaccinations**: No specific vaccinations are required for Norway, but it's always a good idea to be up-to-date on routine vaccinations.
• **Safety Precautions**: Norway is generally safe, but exercise normal precautions, especially in tourist areas where pickpocketing and petty theft can occur.

Budgeting for Your Norwegian Fjord Cruise

Creating a well-thought-out budget is essential for ensuring a stress-free and enjoyable Norwegian fjord cruise. By planning ahead and accounting for all possible expenses, you can make the most of your trip without worrying about unexpected costs. Here's a detailed guide to help you budget for your Norwegian fjord adventure:

1. Cruise Costs

Cruise Fare:
• Range: The cost of a Norwegian fjord cruise can vary widely depending on the cruise line, itinerary, cabin type, and travel dates. Expect to pay anywhere from $1,000 to $5,000 per person for a 7• to 14-day cruise.
• Tips: Book early to take advantage of early-bird discounts, and consider traveling during the shoulder seasons (spring and autumn) for lower fares.

Inclusions:

• Included: Most cruise fares include accommodation, meals, entertainment, and access to onboard facilities.
• Extra Costs: Be aware of additional costs such as specialty dining, alcoholic beverages, spa treatments, and shore excursions.

2. Flights and Transportation

Flights:
• **Range**: Round-trip airfare to Norway can range from $500 to $1,500 per person, depending on your departure city and the time of year.
• Tips: Use flight comparison websites to find the best deals, and consider booking flights several months in advance for better prices.

Ground Transportation:
• Costs: Budget for transportation to and from the airport, cruise terminal, and any additional transfers. This may include taxis, shuttles, or public transportation.
• Tips: Research the most cost-effective transportation options and consider using public transit when possible.

3. Accommodation

Pre• and Post-Cruise Accommodation:
• Range: Hotel prices in Norwegian cities like Bergen and Oslo can vary widely. Expect to pay between $100 and $300 per night for a mid-range hotel.
• Tips: Book accommodation early, especially if you're traveling during peak seasons, and consider staying in budget-friendly options like guesthouses or hostels.

4. Food and Dining

Onboard Dining:
• **Included**: Most meals are included in your cruise fare, but specialty dining venues may have additional charges.
• **Tips**: Take advantage of the included dining options and budget for occasional splurges at specialty restaurants.

Dining Ashore:
• Range: Meals in Norway can be expensive, with average prices ranging from $15 to $30 for lunch and $20 to $50 for dinner per person.
• Tips: Opt for local cafes and bakeries for budget-friendly meals and consider picnicking with items from local markets.

5. Shore Excursions and Activities

Range: Shore excursions can range from $50 to $300 per person, depending on the activity and duration.

Tips:
• Book Wisely: While cruise lines offer convenient and curated excursions, they can be pricey. Consider booking independently or exploring on your own to save money.
• Free Activities: Many ports offer free or low-cost activities, such as hiking, exploring local towns, and visiting museums.

6. Travel Insurance

Range: Travel insurance costs can vary based on coverage and duration, but expect to pay around 5% to 10% of your total trip cost.

Tips: Choose a comprehensive travel insurance plan that covers medical emergencies, trip cancellations, lost or stolen belongings, and other unexpected events.

7. Miscellaneous Expenses

Souvenirs and Shopping:
• Range: Budget for souvenirs, local crafts, and gifts. Prices can vary, but a safe estimate is $50 to $200.
• Tips: Shop at local markets for unique and affordable items, and set a souvenir budget to avoid overspending.

Gratuities:
• Range: Many cruise lines have a daily gratuity charge ranging from $10 to $15 per person, per day. This is often automatically added to your onboard account.
• Tips: Check if gratuities are included in your cruise fare and budget accordingly.

Emergency Fund:
• **Range**: Set aside an emergency fund for unexpected expenses, such as medical emergencies or unforeseen changes in travel plans. A safe estimate is $200 to $500.

Creating a detailed budget for your Norwegian fjord cruise ensures that you can enjoy your trip without financial stress. By accounting for all possible expenses, from cruise fares and flights to dining and excursions, you can make informed decisions and manage your finances effectively.

Chapter 3. Pre-Departure Preparation

Packing Essentials for a Norwegian Fjord Cruise

Embarking on a Norwegian fjord cruise promises breathtaking scenery, outdoor adventures, and unforgettable experiences. Packing wisely can enhance your trip and ensure you're prepared for all the unique opportunities this journey offers. Here's a comprehensive list of essentials to help you pack for your fjord cruise:

Clothing

Layering is Key:
• **Base Layers**: Start with moisture-wicking base layers to keep you dry and comfortable. Long-sleeve shirts and thermal tops are great options.
• **Mid Layers**: Add insulating mid layers such as fleece jackets or wool sweaters for warmth.
• Outer Layers: Bring a waterproof and windproof jacket to protect against rain and wind. A good quality raincoat is essential for fjord weather.
• **Trousers**: Pack comfortable trousers that are suitable for hiking and outdoor activities. Quick-drying pants are a plus.
• **Casual Wear**: Include a few casual outfits for onboard dining and relaxing. Comfortable jeans, shirts, and sweaters are perfect for this.

• **Dressier Attire**: Some cruises have formal nights, so pack a dress or a suit if you plan to participate in these events.

Footwear:
• **Comfortable Walking Shoes**: Bring a pair of sturdy, comfortable walking shoes or hiking boots for excursions and exploring.
• **Waterproof Footwear**: Waterproof shoes or boots are essential for wet conditions and activities like kayaking.
• **Casual Shoes**: Pack a pair of casual shoes for onboard activities and dinners.

Accessories

Sun Protection:
• **Sun Hat:** A wide-brimmed hat is essential for protecting your face from the sun.
• **Sunglasses**: Bring a good pair of UV-protective sunglasses to shield your eyes from the bright sun.
• **Sunscreen**: Pack a high SPF sunscreen (at least SPF 30) and apply it regularly, even on cloudy days.

Cold Weather Accessories:
• **Beanie or Hat**: A warm beanie or hat is essential for cooler days and evenings.
• **Gloves**: Bring a pair of insulated gloves to keep your hands warm during outdoor activities.
• **Scarf or Neck Gaiter**: A scarf or neck gaiter will keep you warm and protect against the wind.

Other Essentials:
• **Reusable Water Bottle**: Stay hydrated by bringing a reusable water bottle that you can refill throughout the day.

• **Daypack**: A small backpack or daypack is useful for carrying essentials during shore excursions and hikes.
• **Binoculars**: Pack a pair of binoculars to fully appreciate the stunning landscapes and spot wildlife from a distance.

Outdoor and Adventure Gear

Hiking and Exploring:
• **Walking Poles**: If you plan on hiking, bring a pair of collapsible walking poles for added stability and support.
• **Swimsuit**: Some fjord cruises offer opportunities for swimming or using the onboard pool and hot tub.
• **Waterproof Dry Bag**: A waterproof dry bag can keep your valuables safe and dry during water-based activities.

Photography and Gadgets:
• **Camera**: Capture the beauty of the fjords with a good camera. Bring extra memory cards and batteries.
• **Smartphone and Charger**: Don't forget your smartphone for photos, navigation, and staying connected. Bring a portable charger as well.

Health and Safety

First Aid Kit:
• **Basic Items**: Include band-aids, antiseptic wipes, pain relievers, motion sickness medication, and any prescription medications you may need.
• **Hand Sanitizer**: Pack hand sanitizer for quick and easy hand cleaning.

Travel Insurance:

• **Documents**: Bring copies of your travel insurance policy and any important health documents.

Emergency Fund:
• **Cash:** Carry a small amount of cash in local currency for small purchases and tips.
• **Credit Cards**: Bring your credit cards for larger expenses and emergencies.

Important Documents

Travel Documents:
• **Passport**: Ensure your passport is valid for at least six months beyond your travel dates.
• **Visa**: If required, bring your Schengen visa and any other necessary travel documents.
• **Travel Itinerary**: Have a copy of your travel itinerary, including cruise confirmation, flight details, and accommodation reservations.
• **Copies of Important Documents**: Keep copies of your passport, travel insurance, and other important documents in a separate location from the originals.

Packing for a Norwegian fjord cruise requires careful consideration to ensure you're prepared for the diverse weather conditions and activities. By following this comprehensive packing list, you can enjoy your journey to the fullest, from hiking scenic trails to relaxing onboard and exploring charming villages.

Travel Insurance and Health Tips

Ensuring you have comprehensive travel insurance and following health tips are essential for a safe and enjoyable Norwegian fjord cruise. Here's a detailed guide to help you prepare:

Travel Insurance

Why It's Important:
Travel insurance provides coverage for a range of unexpected events, from medical emergencies and trip cancellations to lost luggage and travel delays. Having travel insurance gives you peace of mind and financial protection during your trip.

Types of Coverage:
• **Medical Emergencies**: Covers the cost of medical treatment, hospitalization, and emergency evacuation. This is especially important when traveling in remote areas like the fjords.
• **Trip Cancellation/Interruption:** Reimburses you for non-refundable trip costs if you need to cancel or interrupt your trip due to covered reasons (e.g., illness, family emergency, natural disasters).
• **Lost or Delayed Baggage**: Provides compensation for lost, stolen, or delayed luggage and personal belongings.
• **Travel Delays**: Covers additional expenses incurred due to travel delays, such as accommodation and meals.
• **Accidental Death and Dismemberment**: Provides financial compensation in the event of accidental death or serious injury during your trip.

Choosing the Right Plan:
• **Comprehensive Coverage**: Opt for a comprehensive travel insurance plan that includes medical, trip

cancellation/interruption, and baggage coverage.

• **Adventure Activities**: Ensure the plan covers adventure activities you plan to participate in, such as hiking, kayaking, and glacier exploration.

• **Pre-Existing Conditions**: Check if the policy covers pre-existing medical conditions. Some insurers offer waivers for pre-existing conditions if you purchase the policy within a certain timeframe after booking your trip.

Having comprehensive travel insurance has saved me from potential financial setbacks on several occasions. From covering medical expenses during an unexpected illness to reimbursing me for a delayed flight, travel insurance has provided invaluable peace of mind.

Health Tips

Stay Hydrated:

• **Drink Plenty of Water:** Dehydration can occur even in cooler climates, so make sure to drink plenty of water throughout the day.

• **Bring a Reusable Water Bottle**: Refill it regularly to stay hydrated during shore excursions and onboard activities.

Protect Yourself from the Sun:

• **Use Sunscreen**: Apply sunscreen with at least SPF 30, even on cloudy days. Reapply every two hours, especially if you're sweating or swimming.

• **Wear a Hat and Sunglasses**: Protect your face and eyes from the sun's rays by wearing a wide-brimmed hat and UV-protective sunglasses.

Prevent Motion Sickness:

• **Medications**: If you're prone to motion sickness, bring over-the-counter medications like Dramamine or Bonine. Consider wearing acupressure wristbands for additional relief.

• **Cabin Location**: Choose a cabin in the middle of the ship and on a lower deck, where there's less motion.

Practice Good Hygiene:

• **Hand Sanitizer**: Carry hand sanitizer and use it frequently, especially before meals and after touching common surfaces.

• **Wash Hands**: Wash your hands with soap and water regularly to prevent the spread of germs.

Stay Active:

• **Exercise**: Take advantage of onboard fitness facilities, such as the gym, jogging track, and swimming pool, to stay active.

• **Stretch**: Incorporate stretching exercises into your daily routine to prevent stiffness from long periods of sitting.

Be Prepared for Emergencies:

• **First Aid Kit**: Bring a basic first aid kit with band-aids, antiseptic wipes, pain relievers, motion sickness medication, and any prescription medications you may need.

• **Know Emergency Numbers**: Familiarize yourself with the ship's emergency procedures and know the location of medical facilities onboard.

During my travels, I always prioritize staying healthy and prepared. Simple practices like staying hydrated, using sunscreen, and carrying a first aid kit have helped me enjoy my adventures to the fullest. Being mindful of health tips ensures a safe and pleasant journey.

Comprehensive travel insurance and following essential health tips are crucial for a safe and enjoyable Norwegian fjord cruise. By being well-prepared and mindful of your health, you can fully immerse yourself in the beauty and adventure of the fjords without worry.

Sustainable Travel Practices for a Norwegian Fjord Cruise

Embracing sustainable travel practices is essential for preserving the natural beauty and unique ecosystems of the Norwegian fjords. By being mindful of our environmental impact and making conscious choices, we can help protect this stunning destination for future generations. Here's a detailed guide to sustainable travel practices for your fjord cruise:

1. Reduce Plastic Use

Why: Single-use plastics are a major source of pollution and can harm marine life. Reducing plastic use helps protect the pristine waters and ecosystems of the fjords.

Practices:
• **Bring Reusable Items:** Pack reusable water bottles, shopping bags, and containers to minimize plastic waste. Many cruise lines and local businesses in Norway support eco-friendly practices and offer alternatives to single-use plastics.

• **Say No to Straws**: Opt for reusable or biodegradable straws, or simply go without. Many restaurants and cafes in the fjords offer eco-friendly straw options.

I vividly remember sipping a refreshing drink through a biodegradable straw while gazing at the majestic fjords. The simple act of using eco-friendly alternatives made me feel like I was contributing to the preservation of this beautiful destination.

2. Practice Responsible Wildlife Viewing

Why: The Norwegian fjords are home to diverse and fragile ecosystems. Respecting wildlife and their habitats ensures that these creatures can thrive in their natural environment.

Practices:
• **Keep a Safe Distance**: Observe wildlife from a safe and respectful distance. Avoid approaching or touching animals, as this can stress them and disrupt their natural behavior.
• **Do Not Feed Wildlife**: Feeding wildlife can be harmful to their health and can lead to dependency on human-provided food. Admire animals in their natural habitat without interfering.

Watching a pod of dolphins playfully swim alongside our boat was a magical moment. Maintaining a respectful distance allowed us to appreciate their beauty without causing any harm.

3. Choose Eco-Friendly Accommodations

Why: Staying at eco-friendly accommodations supports businesses that prioritize sustainability and environmental conservation.

Practices:
• **Look for Green Certifications**: Choose accommodations with certifications such as Nordic Swan Ecolabel, which indicate a commitment to sustainable practices.
• **Support Local**: Opt for locally-owned accommodations that prioritize sustainability and contribute to the local economy.

Staying at an eco-friendly hotel with stunning views of the fjords was a highlight of my trip. The hotel's commitment to sustainability, from energy-efficient lighting to locally-sourced meals, made my stay even more memorable.

4. Conserve Water and Energy

Why: Water and energy conservation are crucial for protecting the environment and reducing resource consumption.

Practices:
• **Reuse Towels and Linens**: Many hotels and cruise lines offer the option to reuse towels and linens to reduce water and energy use. Take advantage of this option to minimize your environmental impact.
• **Turn Off Lights and Appliances**: Be mindful of your energy use by turning off lights, air conditioning, and appliances when not in use.

Simple actions like turning off the lights when leaving the room or reusing towels made me more conscious of my environmental footprint. It felt rewarding to know that these small steps were helping to conserve resources.

5. Participate in Eco-Friendly Activities

Why: Choosing eco-friendly activities and tours supports sustainable tourism and helps protect the environment.

Practices:
• **Choose Sustainable Tours**: Look for tour operators that prioritize sustainability and environmental conservation. Many offer eco-friendly activities such as hiking, kayaking, and wildlife viewing.
• **Leave No Trace**: Follow the Leave No Trace principles by minimizing your impact on the environment. Pack out all trash, stay on designated trails, and respect wildlife and their habitats.

Hiking along a scenic trail with a knowledgeable guide who shared insights about the local ecosystem was an enriching experience. The guide's passion for conservation inspired me to be more mindful of my impact on the environment.

6. Support Local Conservation Efforts

Why: Supporting local conservation efforts helps protect the natural beauty and biodiversity of the fjords.

Practices:
• **Volunteer**: Consider volunteering with local conservation organizations or participating in clean-up events. Your efforts can make a positive impact on the environment.

• **Donate**: Support local conservation initiatives by making a donation to organizations dedicated to protecting the fjords' ecosystems.

Participating in a beach clean-up event along the fjord shores was a humbling and rewarding experience. Working alongside locals to remove litter and debris made me feel connected to the community and the environment.

7. Reduce Carbon Footprint

Why: Reducing your carbon footprint helps mitigate climate change and its impact on the environment.

Practices:
• **Use Public Transportation**: Opt for public transportation, biking, or walking instead of driving. The fjord regions offer excellent public transit options and scenic bike paths.
• **Offset Carbon Emissions**: Consider purchasing carbon offsets to compensate for the carbon emissions from your travel.

Taking a scenic bike ride along the fjord coast was a highlight of my trip. The fresh air, stunning views, and sense of adventure made it a memorable and eco-friendly way to explore the area.

By embracing sustainable travel practices, you can help protect the natural beauty and unique ecosystems of the Norwegian fjords. From reducing plastic use and conserving resources to supporting local conservation efforts and choosing eco-friendly activities, there are many ways to make a positive impact.

Chapter 4. Ports of Call: Exploring the Highlights

Bergen: Gateway to the Fjords

Must-See Attractions

1. Bryggen (The Hanseatic Wharf): This UNESCO World Heritage site is a colorful row of wooden houses along the harbor. Stroll through the narrow alleyways, visit museums, and shop for unique souvenirs. The history and charm of Bryggen will transport you back to the days of the Hanseatic League.

2. Fløibanen Funicular: Take a ride up Mount Fløyen for breathtaking panoramic views of Bergen and the surrounding fjords. The funicular ride itself is an adventure, and once you reach the top, you can explore hiking trails, a café, and even a troll forest for kids.

3. Bergenhus Fortress: One of the oldest and best-preserved fortresses in Norway. Explore the medieval Håkon's Hall and the Rosenkrantz Tower, both offering a glimpse into Bergen's storied past.

4. Troldhaugen: The former home of composer Edvard Grieg. Tour the house, enjoy a concert in the concert hall, and wander through the beautiful gardens overlooking Lake Nordås.

5. KODE Museums: A collection of four museums showcasing art, design, and music. From Edvard Munch's paintings to contemporary art, KODE has something for every art lover.

6. Ulriken Cable Car: Ride the cable car to the top of Mount Ulriken, the highest of Bergen's seven mountains. The views from the top are spectacular, and the ride itself is an exhilarating experience.

Local Cuisine and Dining Options

1. Bryggeloftet & Stuene: Located in Bryggen, this restaurant offers traditional Norwegian cuisine with a modern twist. Enjoy dishes like Bergen fish soup and fresh seafood while soaking in the historic atmosphere.

2. Lysverket: A Michelin-starred restaurant located in the KODE 4 art museum. Known for redefining Nordic cuisine, Lysverket offers a modern Norwegian menu with a strong emphasis on local seafood.

3. Frescohallen: Situated in the historic Bergen Børs Hotel, Frescohallen combines local produce with international flair. Highlights include lobster pasta, salmon from Sotra, and beef tartare with Worcestershire sauce.

4. Cornelius Seafood Restaurant: Located by the harbor, this restaurant offers a fantastic seafood experience. Try freshly caught salmon or king crab while enjoying the vibrant atmosphere.

5. Enhjørningen Seafood Restaurant: Another excellent seafood option, Enhjørningen is known for its delicious and fresh seafood dishes.

Shopping and Souvenirs

1. Bryggen Shops: The historic area of Bryggen is filled with charming shops selling everything from troll figurines to hand-knitted garments. Don't miss the only year-round Christmas shop in Norway, Julehuset, which offers a variety of festive decorations and gifts.

2. Arven Gold & Silverfactory: Visit this shop to see silversmiths at work and browse a unique selection of handcrafted silverware and jewelry. It's a great place to find a lasting souvenir.

3. Oleana: Known for its colorful and hand-knitted garments, Oleana carries the history and traditions of Bergen. These unique garments make for wonderful gifts and keepsakes.

4. The Fish Market: Located in the heart of the city, the Fish Market offers fresh seafood and local delicacies. It's a great place to pick up some edible souvenirs and enjoy the bustling atmosphere.

Why Visit Bergen?

Bergen is a city that seamlessly blends natural beauty with rich history and vibrant culture.

From the stunning fjords to the charming wooden houses of Bryggen, there's something for everyone to enjoy. The local cuisine is a treat for food lovers, and the shopping options offer unique and authentic souvenirs. Whether you're hiking up Mount Fløyen, exploring the KODE museums, or enjoying a seafood dinner by the harbor, Bergen is a destination that will leave you enchanted and eager to return.

Navigating Bergen

transportation system, including buses and the funicular, is efficient and convenient. For those who enjoy biking, Bergen offers scenic bike paths that allow you to take in the beauty of the city and its surroundings. Taxis and car rentals are also available for those who prefer more flexibility in their travel plans.

I remember my first visit to Bergen vividly. The moment I stepped off the train and saw the colorful houses of Bryggen, I knew I was in a special place. The friendly locals, the delicious seafood, and the breathtaking views made my stay unforgettable. I spent hours wandering through the narrow alleyways of Bryggen, admiring the craftsmanship of the local artisans and savoring every bite of the fresh seafood. The hike up Mount Fløyen was challenging but rewarding, with the panoramic views making every step worth it. And the cozy atmosphere of the local cafes and restaurants made me feel right at home.

Bergen is a city that captures the essence of Norway's natural beauty and cultural heritage. Whether you're a nature lover, a history buff, or a food enthusiast, Bergen has something to

Bergen is a compact city, making it easy to explore on foot. The city's public offer. So, if you're ever in Norway, make sure to add Bergen to your travel itinerary. You won't regret it!

Ålesund: Art Nouveau City

Architectural Highlights

Ålesund is renowned for its Art Nouveau architecture, which emerged after a devastating fire in 1904. The city was rebuilt with vibrant pastel-colored buildings adorned with intricate details, turrets, and towers. Some key highlights include:

• **Jugendstilsenteret (The Art Nouveau Centre):** A museum dedicated to the city's unique architectural style.

• **Aksla Viewpoint**: Offers panoramic views of the city and its surroundings.

• **Arbeideren Kulturhus**: A cultural center that was originally a theater and now hosts concerts and exhibitions.

Outdoor Adventures

Ålesund is surrounded by stunning natural landscapes, offering a variety of outdoor activities:

• **Hiking**: Climb Aksla Mountain for breathtaking views.

• **Fjord Cruises**: Explore the Geirangerfjord and Hjørundfjord for scenic beauty and wildlife watching.

• **Kayaking and Surfing**: Enjoy water sports in the surrounding fjords.

• **Skiing and Snowboarding**: The Sunnmøre Alps provide excellent slopes for winter sports.

Cultural Experiences

The city also offers rich cultural experiences:
• **Norwegian Aquarium**: A family-friendly attraction showcasing Norway's aquatic ecosystem.
• **Local Cuisine**: Try fresh seafood at local restaurants like Fisketorget and Bro Restaurant.
• **Concerts and Theaters**: Enjoy performances at venues like Terminalen Byscene and Teaterfabrikken.
• **Street Art and Galleries**: Explore local art at KHÅK Kunsthall and take a walk down Moloveien.

Why Visit Ålesund?

Ålesund is a city that effortlessly combines architectural beauty with outdoor adventure and rich cultural experiences. The unique Art Nouveau buildings give the city a distinct and charming character, making it a visual feast for architecture enthusiasts. The surrounding natural landscapes offer endless opportunities for outdoor activities, from hiking and fjord cruises to skiing and kayaking. The vibrant cultural scene, including the aquarium, local cuisine, and performing arts, ensures that there's something for everyone to enjoy.

Navigating Ålesund

Ålesund is a compact and walkable city, making it easy to explore on foot. Public transportation, including buses and ferries, is efficient and convenient for reaching outlying areas and attractions. For those who prefer more flexibility, taxis and car rentals are also available.

I remember my first visit to Ålesund with great fondness. The city's vibrant architecture immediately captured my heart, and I spent hours wandering through the streets, marveling at the intricate details of the buildings. The hike up Aksla Mountain was both challenging and rewarding, with panoramic views that took my breath away. I indulged in fresh seafood at local restaurants and enjoyed a fascinating visit to the aquarium. The city's blend of natural beauty, rich culture, and friendly locals made my stay truly unforgettable.

Ålesund is a city that captures the essence of Norway's natural beauty and cultural heritage. Whether you're an architecture enthusiast, an outdoor adventurer, or a culture lover, Ålesund has something to offer. If you're ever in Norway, make sure to add Ålesund to your travel itinerary—you won't regret it!

I hope this guide inspires you and your friends to visit Ålesund and experience all the wonders this beautiful city has to offer.

Geiranger: Jewel of the Fjords

Geiranger, often referred to as the "Jewel of the Fjords," is a breathtakingly beautiful destination that offers stunning landscapes, dramatic waterfalls, and unparalleled fjord views. This charming village, nestled at the end of the Geirangerfjord, is a must-visit for anyone exploring Norway's natural wonders. Let's delve into the highlights of Geiranger:

Scenic Overlooks and Hikes

1. Dalsnibba Mountain Plateau:

• **Why Visit**: Standing at an elevation of 1,500 meters, Dalsnibba offers an unmatched panoramic view of Geirangerfjord, surrounded by snow-capped peaks and lush valleys.

• Reaching the top of Dalsnibba felt like standing on top of the world. The sweeping vistas of the fjord below and the mountains around were awe-inspiring. It's a sight that remains etched in memory.

2. Flydalsjuvet:

• **Why Visit**: This iconic viewpoint provides one of the most photographed panoramas in Norway. The sight of the fjord, framed by rugged cliffs, is simply spectacular.

• Sitting on the famous "Flydalsjuvet rock" gave me a profound sense of peace. The view was both humbling and exhilarating.

3. Skageflå Farm Hike:

• **Why Visit**: This historic mountain farm, perched on a cliff, offers a hike that combines natural beauty with cultural heritage. The trail provides magnificent views of the fjord and waterfalls.

• The hike to Skageflå was challenging but incredibly rewarding. Walking through lush forests and seeing the fjord from above was an adventure worth every step.

Waterfall Wonders

1. Seven Sisters Waterfall:

• **Why Visit**: This famous waterfall consists of seven separate streams cascading down a 250-meter cliff. The sight is mesmerizing, especially when viewed from a boat or the opposite side of the fjord.

• Watching the Seven Sisters waterfall was like witnessing nature's elegance in motion. The sheer force and beauty of the cascading water were captivating.

2. Suitor (Friaren) Waterfall:

• **Why Visit**: Located directly opposite the Seven Sisters, the Suitor waterfall is said to be "courting" the sisters. This charming legend adds to the allure of the falls.

• The playful tale of the Suitor waterfall courting the Seven Sisters added a layer of whimsy to the already enchanting scenery. It was delightful to learn local folklore while admiring the falls.

3. Bridal Veil Waterfall (Brudesløret):

• **Why Visit**: This delicate waterfall appears as a fine veil when backlit by the sun, giving it its romantic name. It's a picturesque sight, especially during the spring melt.

• The Bridal Veil waterfall looked like a translucent curtain of water, shimmering in the sunlight. The serene beauty of this waterfall was a highlight of my visit.

Geirangerfjord Cruise Excursions

1. Geirangerfjord Sightseeing Cruise:

• **Why Visit**: A fjord cruise is the best way to experience the dramatic beauty of Geirangerfjord up close. The cruises often pass by the majestic waterfalls and offer commentary on the region's history and legends.

• Gliding through the calm waters of Geirangerfjord on a sightseeing cruise was an unforgettable experience. The towering cliffs, cascading waterfalls, and the serene beauty of the fjord created a sense of wonder and tranquility.

2. Rib Boat Safari:
• **Why Visit**: For an adrenaline-pumping adventure, a RIB (Rigid Inflatable Boat) safari provides a thrilling way to explore the fjord. The high-speed ride and close-up views of the waterfalls and wildlife are exhilarating.
• The RIB boat safari was a heart-pounding adventure. Speeding through the fjord and getting up close to the waterfalls was an experience that left me breathless and exhilarated.

3. Kayaking Tours:
• **Why Visit**: Kayaking in Geirangerfjord offers a peaceful and immersive way to connect with nature. Paddle at your own pace and enjoy the serenity of the fjord, with the opportunity to spot seals and eagles.
• Kayaking in Geirangerfjord was a deeply calming experience. The stillness of the water, the sound of the paddle slicing through the fjord, and the sight of eagles soaring above made it a truly meditative journey.

Geiranger is a destination that perfectly encapsulates the breathtaking beauty and serene tranquility of the Norwegian fjords. From awe-inspiring scenic overlooks and adventurous hikes to the mesmerizing waterfalls and unforgettable fjord cruises, Geiranger offers a wealth of experiences that will leave you enchanted and longing to return.

Flam: Railway Adventures

Flam, nestled in the heart of Norway's fjord country, is a charming village known for its breathtaking landscapes, unique railway journey, and delightful local experiences. Let's explore what makes Flam a must-visit destination:

Flam Railway Journey

The Flam Railway (Flåmsbana):
• **Why Visit:** The Flam Railway is one of the most scenic train journeys in the world, offering a mesmerizing ride through the Norwegian mountains. The 20-kilometer (12.4-mile) journey takes you from the end of Aurlandsfjord in Flam to the high mountain station of Myrdal.
• **Scenic Highlights**: The journey takes you through lush valleys, alongside roaring waterfalls, and past snow-capped peaks. Notable stops include the Kjosfossen waterfall, where you can disembark to take photos and experience the thundering power of the falls up close.
• Riding the Flam Railway was an unforgettable experience. As the train wound its way through the dramatic landscapes, I was captivated by the ever-changing scenery. The stop at Kjosfossen waterfall was particularly magical, with the mist and roar of the water creating a truly immersive experience.

Activities and Excursions

1. Fjord Safari:
• **Why Visit**: Explore the stunning Aurlandsfjord and Nærøyfjord by RIB (Rigid Inflatable Boat). This thrilling safari offers close-up views of the fjords, wildlife, and cascading waterfalls.

• The fjord safari was an exhilarating adventure. Speeding through the fjords and witnessing the sheer cliffs and waterfalls from the water was awe-inspiring. The knowledgeable guides shared fascinating insights about the fjord's history and wildlife.

2. Hiking and Biking:

• **Why Visit**: Flam offers a variety of hiking and biking trails that showcase the region's natural beauty. Popular routes include the hike to Brekkefossen waterfall and the Rallarvegen bike trail.

• Hiking to Brekkefossen was a rewarding experience. The trail led me through lush forests and offered stunning views of the valley and fjord below. The sight of the waterfall cascading down the mountainside was well worth the effort.

3. Stegastein Viewpoint:

• **Why Visit**: This panoramic viewing platform extends 30 meters (98 feet) out from the mountainside, offering breathtaking views of the Aurlandsfjord and surrounding mountains.

• Standing on the Stegastein Viewpoint felt like floating above the fjord. The sweeping vistas were nothing short of spectacular, and it was a perfect spot for capturing memorable photos.

4. Fjord Cruises:

• **Why Visit**: Embark on a leisurely fjord cruise to fully appreciate the stunning landscapes of Aurlandsfjord and Nærøyfjord. These UNESCO World Heritage sites are known for their dramatic beauty and serene waters.

• The fjord cruise was a serene and picturesque experience. Gliding through the calm waters, surrounded by towering cliffs and lush greenery, felt like stepping into a fairy tale.

Local Delicacies

1. Ægir BrewPub:

• **Why Visit**: Located in Flam, Ægir BrewPub offers a unique dining experience with a Viking-inspired atmosphere. The pub serves craft beers brewed on-site and a menu featuring local ingredients.

• Dining at Ægir BrewPub was a delightful experience. The rustic decor and cozy ambiance made me feel like I was dining in a Viking longhouse. The craft beers were exceptional, and the dishes, such as the reindeer burger, were flavorful and well-prepared.

2. Flåm Bakery:

• **Why Visit**: This charming bakery offers a variety of freshly baked goods, including pastries, bread, and cakes. It's a perfect spot for a quick snack or breakfast before embarking on your adventures.

• The aroma of freshly baked goods drew me into Flåm Bakery. I indulged in a delicious cinnamon bun and a cup of coffee, which provided the perfect start to my day in Flam.

3. Local Farms and Markets:

• **Why Visit**: Explore the local farms and markets to taste and purchase fresh produce, cheeses, and other regional specialties. These markets offer a glimpse into the local agricultural traditions.

• Visiting a local farm was a highlight of my trip. I sampled fresh goat cheese and strawberries, which were bursting with flavor.

The farmers were friendly and eager to share stories about their produce and way of life.

Flam is a destination that combines natural beauty, thrilling adventures, and delightful local experiences. Whether you're taking a scenic ride on the Flam Railway, exploring the fjords on a safari or cruise, hiking to breathtaking viewpoints, or savoring local delicacies, Flam offers something for everyone. This charming village is a gateway to the wonders of Norway's fjord country and is sure to leave you with lasting memories.

Chapter 5. Onboard Cruise Experience

Life on a Fjord Cruise Ship

Embarking on a fjord cruise is akin to stepping into a floating sanctuary that carries you through some of the most breathtaking landscapes on Earth. The days are filled with awe-inspiring vistas, enriching activities, and a sense of tranquility that only comes from being surrounded by nature's grandeur. Allow me to take you on a journey through life on a fjord cruise ship, drawing from my own unforgettable experiences.

Morning Bliss

Sunrise Over the Fjords:
• Waking up to the first light of dawn gently illuminating the fjords is a sight that will stay with you forever. I remember standing on my private balcony, wrapped in a cozy blanket, as the ship glided silently through the still waters. The mountains, shrouded in mist, slowly revealed their majestic beauty as the sun rose, casting a golden glow over the landscape. It was a moment of pure serenity, and I felt a deep connection to the natural world.

Breakfast with a View:
• One of the highlights of my mornings was enjoying breakfast in the ship's panoramic dining room. With floor-to-ceiling windows, every seat offered a stunning view of the fjords. I indulged in a hearty Scandinavian breakfast, featuring smoked salmon, fresh fruits, and a variety of pastries. Sipping my coffee while watching the ever-changing scenery was a delightful way to start the day.

Daytime Adventures

Shore Excursions:
• Each day brought a new port of call and the promise of adventure. One day, I found myself hiking to the breathtaking Briksdal Glacier, the icy blue expanse a stark contrast to the lush green valley below. On another, I explored the charming village of Geiranger, with its quaint houses and cascading waterfalls. Each excursion offered a unique glimpse into the rich culture and natural beauty of Norway.

Onboard Activities:
• When not exploring ashore, the ship offered a plethora of activities to keep us engaged. I attended informative lectures about Norwegian history and geography, participated in a cooking class where we learned to make traditional Norwegian dishes, and even tried my hand at watercolor painting, inspired by the stunning landscapes surrounding us. The onboard library, stocked with books about the region, became a favorite spot for quiet reflection.

Afternoon Relaxation

Spa and Wellness:

• After a morning of exploration, indulging in the ship's spa was a luxurious treat. The spa offered a range of treatments, from soothing massages to invigorating facials. I opted for a hot stone massage, which left me feeling completely relaxed and rejuvenated. The spa's relaxation lounge, with its floor-to-ceiling windows, provided a tranquil space to unwind while gazing at the fjord scenery.

Scenic Cruising:

• One of the most memorable aspects of the cruise was the scenic sailing through the narrow fjords. I spent countless hours on the ship's deck, bundled up in warm layers, as we navigated through the towering cliffs and cascading waterfalls. The captain's commentary added depth to the experience, sharing fascinating stories and facts about the fjords and their history. The highlight was sailing through the UNESCO-listed Geirangerfjord, with its dramatic landscapes and iconic Seven Sisters waterfall.

Evening Elegance

Gourmet Dining:

• Dinner onboard was a culinary delight, with a menu that showcased the flavors of the region. One evening, I savored a dish of fresh cod, paired with locally sourced vegetables and a creamy dill sauce. The elegant dining room, with its refined decor and attentive service, created a perfect ambiance for a memorable meal. For a more intimate experience, I dined at the specialty restaurant, where the chef's tasting menu took me on a gastronomic journey through Norway's culinary heritage.

Entertainment and Nightlife:

• Evenings on the ship were filled with entertainment and camaraderie. I enjoyed live performances by talented musicians, from classical piano recitals to traditional Norwegian folk music. The ship's lounge, with its cozy seating and warm atmosphere, became a favorite spot for evening cocktails and conversation with fellow travelers. One of the highlights was a special "Norwegian Night," where the crew donned traditional costumes, and we were treated to a lively show featuring traditional dance and music.

Nighttime Serenity

Stargazing on Deck:

• As the night fell, the ship's deck offered a serene space for stargazing. Wrapped in a warm blanket, I marveled at the clear night sky, unpolluted by city lights. The sight of the stars reflecting on the calm waters of the fjord was magical. Occasionally, we were fortunate enough to witness the ethereal beauty of the Northern Lights, their shimmering colors dancing across the sky in a mesmerizing display.

Peaceful Slumber:

• Retiring to my cabin each night, I felt a deep sense of contentment. The gentle rocking of the ship and the distant sound of the water created a soothing lullaby. My cabin, with its plush bedding and cozy decor, provided a perfect sanctuary for a restful night's sleep. Each morning, I woke up refreshed and eager to embrace another day of exploration and adventure.

Life on a fjord cruise ship is a harmonious blend of adventure, relaxation, and indulgence.

From the awe-inspiring landscapes and enriching shore excursions to the luxurious onboard amenities and delightful dining experiences, every moment is designed to create lasting memories. The camaraderie of fellow travelers, the warmth of the crew, and the profound connection to nature make a fjord cruise an unparalleled journey of discovery.

Dining Options and Culinary Delights

One of the most delightful aspects of a fjord cruise is the variety of dining options and the opportunity to savor Norway's culinary treasures. Whether you're enjoying a casual meal with a view, indulging in gourmet cuisine, or sampling local delicacies, the culinary experiences on board are designed to be memorable and satisfying. Let me take you on a gastronomic journey through the different dining options and culinary delights you can expect on a fjord cruise:

Main Dining Room

Atmosphere:
• The main dining room offers an elegant and spacious setting with large windows providing stunning views of the fjords. The ambiance is refined yet relaxed, making it the perfect place to enjoy leisurely meals while taking in the scenery.

Culinary Highlights:
• **Breakfast**: Start your day with a bountiful buffet featuring a variety of options, from freshly baked pastries and bread to smoked salmon, cheeses, and fresh fruits. There's also a selection of hot dishes, such as scrambled eggs, bacon, and sausages, to satisfy hearty appetites.
• **Lunch**: Lunch in the main dining room often includes a mix of international and Norwegian dishes. You might find dishes like creamy fish soup, open-faced sandwiches, and freshly prepared salads. A highlight is the seafood bar, offering prawns, crab, and other delicacies.
• **Dinner**: Dinner is a multi-course affair, with a menu that changes daily to showcase seasonal ingredients and regional flavors. Expect to enjoy dishes like pan-seared cod with dill sauce, roasted reindeer with lingonberry sauce, and decadent desserts like cloudberry mousse.

• One evening, I savored a beautifully presented dish of pan-seared Arctic char, paired with locally sourced vegetables and a creamy mustard sauce. The flavors were exquisite, and the attentive service made the experience even more enjoyable. As I dined, I couldn't help but be captivated by the view of the fjords bathed in the golden light of the setting sun.

Specialty Restaurants

Atmosphere:
• Specialty restaurants offer an intimate and exclusive dining experience, with a focus on gourmet cuisine and impeccable service. These venues often require reservations and may have an additional fee.

Culinary Highlights:
• **Seafood Grill**: Indulge in the freshest seafood, expertly prepared and served with flair. Highlights include grilled king crab legs,

seared scallops, and lobster tails. The dishes are often paired with fine wines to enhance the dining experience.

• **Nordic Bistro**: This restaurant celebrates the best of Nordic cuisine with a modern twist. Dishes like reindeer carpaccio, cured salmon with dill, and slow-cooked lamb are beautifully presented and bursting with flavor.

• **Chef's Table**: For a truly unique experience, the Chef's Table offers a multi-course tasting menu curated by the executive chef. Each course is paired with carefully selected wines, and the chef often shares insights into the ingredients and preparation techniques.

• Dining at the Chef's Table was a highlight of my cruise. The menu featured a delightful progression of dishes, from a delicate amuse-bouche of smoked trout to a sumptuous main course of venison with wild mushroom risotto. Each course was a work of art, and the wine pairings were perfect. The chef's passion and expertise shone through in every bite.

Casual Dining Options

Atmosphere:
• Casual dining venues offer a relaxed and laid-back atmosphere, perfect for informal meals and snacks. These options are great for days when you prefer a quick bite or a more flexible dining schedule.

Culinary Highlights:
• **Buffet Restaurant**: The buffet offers a wide selection of dishes, from salads and pasta to hot entrees and desserts. It's a great option for those who enjoy variety and the freedom to choose their favorites.

• **Pizzeria**: Enjoy freshly baked pizzas with a variety of toppings, from classic margherita to more adventurous combinations like smoked salmon and capers. The pizzeria often features an open kitchen, allowing you to watch the chefs in action.

• **Cafe and Deli**: The cafe offers a selection of sandwiches, pastries, and light snacks, along with specialty coffees and teas. It's a perfect spot for a mid-morning or afternoon treat.

• One afternoon, I visited the buffet restaurant for a casual lunch. I filled my plate with a colorful array of salads, freshly grilled fish, and a generous helping of creamy potato salad. The quality and variety of the food were impressive, and I appreciated the opportunity to sample a little bit of everything.

Local Delicacies

Savoring the Flavors of Norway:
• A fjord cruise is also an excellent opportunity to sample local delicacies and traditional Norwegian dishes. Many cruise lines incorporate regional specialties into their menus, allowing you to experience the authentic flavors of Norway.

Culinary Highlights:
• **Rakfisk**: This fermented fish dish is a Norwegian delicacy, often served with flatbread, sour cream, and onions. It's a unique taste experience that adventurous eaters won't want to miss.

• **Lutefisk**: A traditional dish made from dried cod that's been soaked in lye, then rehydrated and cooked. It's typically served with boiled potatoes, peas, and bacon.

• **Kjøttkaker**: Norwegian meatballs made from ground beef and pork, seasoned with spices, and served with creamy gravy and mashed potatoes.

• **Krumkake**: A delicate, rolled waffle cookie filled with sweet cream. It's a favorite treat during festive occasions and holidays.

• During a themed "Norwegian Night" on the ship, I had the chance to try rakfisk for the first time. The combination of the tangy fermented fish with the creamy sour cream and crispy flatbread was surprisingly delightful. It was an authentic taste of Norway that added to the richness of my culinary journey.

The dining options and culinary delights on a fjord cruise are an integral part of the overall experience. From elegant multi-course dinners and gourmet specialties to casual meals and local delicacies, the variety and quality of the food ensure that every meal is a memorable event. The opportunity to savor traditional Norwegian flavors while enjoying the stunning backdrop of the fjords adds a unique and enriching dimension to the journey.

Entertainment and Activities

A fjord cruise offers a diverse array of entertainment and activities to ensure that every moment of your journey is filled with enjoyment, enrichment, and relaxation. Whether you're looking to immerse yourself in the local culture, stay active, or simply unwind, there's something for everyone. Let me take you through the various entertainment options and activities you can expect on a fjord cruise, drawing from my own experiences to give you a vivid picture of life on board.

Live Performances

Musical Shows and Concerts:
• The ship's main theater often hosts a variety of musical shows and concerts, ranging from classical performances to lively folk music. One evening, I attended a captivating concert by a talented pianist who played a medley of Norwegian compositions. The music, combined with the stunning backdrop of the fjords visible through the theater's large windows, created a truly magical atmosphere.

Dance Performances:
• Traditional dance performances are a highlight of the cruise's entertainment program. I vividly remember an evening of Norwegian folk dancing, where dancers in colorful costumes performed energetic routines to the rhythmic beats of traditional music. The joy and enthusiasm of the performers were infectious, and many of us in the audience couldn't resist tapping our feet along with the music.

Enrichment Programs

Lectures and Talks:
• The cruise offers a series of lectures and talks by experts in various fields, including history, geology, and marine biology. I particularly enjoyed a fascinating lecture on the formation of the fjords, which deepened my appreciation for the landscapes we were exploring. The speaker's passion and knowledge brought the subject to life, and I left with a greater

understanding of the natural wonders around me.

Workshops and Classes:
• Workshops and classes provide opportunities to learn new skills and explore creative pursuits. I took part in a watercolor painting class, inspired by the breathtaking scenery. The instructor guided us through the basics of watercolor techniques, and by the end of the session, I had created my own artistic interpretation of the fjords. It was a rewarding and relaxing way to spend an afternoon.

Outdoor Activities

Hiking and Nature Walks:
• The shore excursions often include guided hikes and nature walks, allowing you to explore the stunning landscapes up close. One of my most memorable hikes was to the Briksdal Glacier, where we walked through lush valleys and alongside glistening rivers before reaching the majestic glacier. The fresh air, the sound of rushing water, and the awe-inspiring views made it an unforgettable adventure.

Kayaking and Water Sports:
• For those who enjoy water sports, kayaking in the fjords is a must-try activity. I had the chance to paddle through the calm waters of Aurlandsfjord, surrounded by towering cliffs and cascading waterfalls. The experience was both serene and exhilarating, offering a unique perspective of the fjords. Other water activities, such as stand-up paddleboarding and fishing, are also available for those looking to stay active.

Wellness and Relaxation

Spa and Wellness Center:
• The ship's spa and wellness center is a haven of relaxation, offering a range of treatments to rejuvenate both body and mind. I treated myself to a soothing hot stone massage, which melted away the tensions of the day. The spa's tranquil ambiance, with its soft lighting and calming music, provided the perfect escape from the hustle and bustle of daily life.

Fitness Center and Classes:
• For those who like to stay active, the fitness center offers state-of-the-art equipment and a variety of fitness classes. I joined a morning yoga session on the ship's deck, where we practiced gentle stretches and poses while enjoying the fresh sea breeze and stunning views of the fjords. It was a refreshing and invigorating way to start the day.

Social and Cultural Activities

Cooking Demonstrations:
• Cooking demonstrations by the ship's chefs offer a delicious insight into Norwegian cuisine. I attended a demonstration on how to make traditional dishes like gravlax (cured salmon) and klippfisk (dried cod). The chefs shared their tips and techniques, and we even got to sample the mouthwatering results. It was a fun and educational experience that added to my culinary repertoire.

Art Exhibitions and Galleries:
• The ship often features art exhibitions and galleries showcasing the work of local artists. I

enjoyed browsing the beautiful paintings and sculptures inspired by the Norwegian landscapes. The art added an extra layer of cultural enrichment to the cruise, and I even purchased a small piece as a keepsake of my journey.

Evening Entertainment

Movie Nights:
• The ship's cinema screens a selection of movies, including documentaries about Norway and classic films. One evening, I watched a documentary about the Northern Lights, which provided fascinating insights into this natural phenomenon. The comfortable seating and high-quality sound made it a great way to unwind after a day of exploration.

Themed Parties and Events:
• Themed parties and events add an element of fun and celebration to the cruise. One memorable night was the "Norwegian Folklore Party," where guests and crew dressed in traditional costumes, and we enjoyed live music, dancing, and Norwegian delicacies. The sense of camaraderie and festive spirit made it a night to remember.

The entertainment and activities on a fjord cruise are designed to cater to a wide range of interests and preferences, ensuring that every moment on board is enjoyable and fulfilling. From live performances and enrichment programs to outdoor adventures and wellness activities, there's something for everyone to enjoy. The diverse offerings allow you to immerse yourself in the local culture, stay active, and relax, all while surrounded by the stunning beauty of the fjords.

Wellness and Relaxation

A fjord cruise is not just about exploring breathtaking landscapes and engaging in exciting activities; it's also an opportunity to indulge in wellness and relaxation. The cruise ships are designed to provide a serene and rejuvenating experience, offering a variety of wellness amenities and relaxation options. Let's delve into the different aspects of wellness and relaxation you can expect on a fjord cruise, enriched with my personal experiences.

Spa and Wellness Center

Luxury Treatments:
• The ship's spa offers a range of luxurious treatments designed to relax and rejuvenate both body and mind. One of my favorite experiences was indulging in a hot stone massage. As the skilled therapist worked on my muscles, the warmth of the stones melted away any tension, leaving me in a state of complete bliss. The soothing ambiance of the spa, with its soft lighting and tranquil music, enhanced the overall experience.

Facials and Skincare:
• I treated myself to a hydrating facial, which left my skin feeling refreshed and glowing. The esthetician used high-quality products and tailored the treatment to my skin type, providing personalized care. It was a perfect way to pamper myself while enjoying the serenity of the fjords.

Aromatherapy and Reflexology:
• Aromatherapy sessions and reflexology treatments are also available in the spa. I

remember an aromatherapy massage where the calming scents of lavender and eucalyptus filled the air, creating a deeply relaxing atmosphere. Reflexology, with its focus on pressure points in the feet, provided a soothing and invigorating experience.

Fitness Center and Classes

State-of-the-Art Equipment:
• The fitness center on the ship is equipped with modern exercise machines, including treadmills, stationary bikes, and weightlifting equipment. I enjoyed starting my mornings with a workout, overlooking the stunning fjord views through the large windows. It was a great way to stay active and energized throughout the cruise.

Group Fitness Classes:
• The ship offers a variety of fitness classes, from yoga and Pilates to high-intensity interval training (HIIT) and aqua aerobics. I joined a morning yoga session on the ship's deck, where we practiced gentle stretches and poses while breathing in the fresh sea air. The instructor's calming voice and the breathtaking backdrop of the fjords made it a truly rejuvenating experience.

Personal Training Sessions:
• For those seeking personalized fitness guidance, the ship's fitness center offers one-on-one training sessions. I scheduled a session with a personal trainer who created a customized workout plan tailored to my fitness goals. The trainer's expertise and motivation helped me stay on track and make the most of my workouts.

Thermal Suite and Relaxation Areas

Thermal Suite:
• The thermal suite is a sanctuary of relaxation, featuring heated loungers, steam rooms, and saunas. I spent an afternoon in the thermal suite, moving between the steam room and the sauna, allowing the heat to relax my muscles and cleanse my skin. The heated loungers, with their ergonomic design, provided a perfect spot to unwind and enjoy the tranquil ambiance.

Hydrotherapy Pool:
• The hydrotherapy pool offers a soothing experience with its warm, bubbling waters and massaging jets. I spent time in the pool, letting the gentle currents and jets relieve any lingering tension. The combination of warm water and stunning views of the fjords made it a truly therapeutic experience.

Quiet Lounges and Reading Rooms:
• For those seeking a peaceful retreat, the ship offers quiet lounges and reading rooms where you can relax with a good book or simply enjoy the silence. I often visited the ship's library, which was stocked with a variety of books and comfortable seating. The cozy atmosphere and the view of the fjords made it an ideal spot for relaxation and reflection.

Outdoor Relaxation

Sun Deck and Pool Area:
• The sun deck and pool area are perfect for soaking up the sun and enjoying the fresh sea breeze. I spent leisurely afternoons lounging by the pool, sipping on refreshing drinks, and taking in the panoramic views of the fjords.

The heated pool and hot tubs provided a relaxing way to unwind after a day of exploration.

Jacuzzis and Hot Tubs:
• The ship's jacuzzis and hot tubs offer a soothing experience with their warm, bubbling waters. I particularly enjoyed the jacuzzis located on the open deck, where I could relax while gazing at the starry night sky. The combination of warm water and the cool evening air created a perfect balance of comfort and relaxation.

Stargazing and Fresh Air:
• One of the most memorable experiences was spending time on the ship's deck at night, stargazing under the clear sky. Wrapped in a cozy blanket, I marveled at the brilliance of the stars reflecting on the calm waters of the fjord. The crisp, fresh air and the sense of tranquility made it a truly magical moment.

Wellness and relaxation are integral parts of the fjord cruise experience. From luxurious spa treatments and invigorating fitness classes to serene thermal suites and peaceful outdoor spaces, the ship offers a variety of options to ensure that you feel rejuvenated and refreshed throughout your journey. The opportunity to unwind and connect with nature while surrounded by the stunning beauty of the fjords adds an extra layer of enrichment to the overall experience.

Chapter 6. Nature and Wildlife

The Flora and Fauna

The Norwegian fjords are not only stunningly beautiful but also home to a rich tapestry of flora and fauna. The unique geological features, diverse ecosystems, and varying climatic conditions create a haven for a wide variety of plant and animal species. Let me take you on a journey through the remarkable flora and fauna of the Norwegian fjords, enriched with personal experiences and observations.

Flora of the Norwegian Fjords

1. Alpine and Sub-Alpine Vegetation:
• **Description**: The high-altitude regions of the fjords are characterized by alpine and sub-alpine vegetation, including hardy grasses, mosses, and low-lying shrubs. These plants are well-adapted to the harsh conditions and short growing seasons.
• Hiking in the mountainous regions of the fjords, I was struck by the resilience and beauty of the alpine flora. The vibrant green mosses and delicate alpine flowers provided a stark contrast to the rugged terrain, creating a picturesque landscape.

2. Coniferous Forests:
• **Description**: The lower slopes of the fjords are often covered in dense coniferous forests, primarily consisting of Norway spruce (Picea abies) and Scots pine (Pinus sylvestris). These forests provide a vital habitat for numerous wildlife species.
• Walking through the serene coniferous forests, I felt a deep sense of tranquility. The towering trees, with their dark green needles, created a canopy that filtered the sunlight, casting dappled shadows on the forest floor. The crisp, pine-scented air was invigorating, and I enjoyed spotting birds and small mammals among the trees.

3. Deciduous Trees and Shrubs:
• **Description**: In the fjord valleys and along the coast, you'll find a mix of deciduous trees and shrubs, including birch (Betula spp.), rowan (Sorbus aucuparia), and willow (Salix spp.). These areas are often lush and vibrant during the growing season.
• During my visit in the spring, the fjord valleys came alive with the sight of blooming birch trees and colorful wildflowers. The delicate white blossoms of the rowan trees added a touch of elegance to the landscape, and the sound of birdsong filled the air.

4. Tundra Vegetation:
• **Description**: In the northern regions and at higher altitudes, tundra vegetation prevails, with hardy plants like lichens, mosses, and low-growing shrubs. These plants are adapted to survive in cold, windy conditions with poor soil.

• Exploring the tundra regions of the fjords felt like stepping into another world. The landscape, covered in a patchwork of lichens and mosses, had a raw, untamed beauty. The resilience of these plants, thriving in such harsh conditions, was truly inspiring.

Fauna of the Norwegian Fjords

1. Marine Life:
• **Whales and Dolphins**:

- Description: The fjords are home to several species of whales and dolphins, including orcas (Orcinus orca), humpback whales (Megaptera novaeangliae), and harbor porpoises (Phocoena phocoena). These marine mammals are often spotted during fjord cruises.

- One of the most thrilling moments of my fjord cruise was spotting a pod of orcas gliding through the water. Their graceful movements and playful behavior were mesmerizing, and it was a privilege to witness these magnificent creatures in their natural habitat.

• **Fish and Invertebrates**:

- Description: The fjord waters are teeming with fish and invertebrates, including cod (Gadus morhua), herring (Clupea harengus), and various species of crabs and shrimp. These species play a crucial role in the fjord's ecosystem.

- While kayaking in the fjords, I marveled at the clarity of the water, which allowed me to see schools of fish swimming below. The diversity of marine life was astounding, and I felt a deep appreciation for the richness of the fjord's underwater world.

2. Birds:

• **Seabirds**:

- **Description**: The fjords are a haven for seabirds, including puffins (Fratercula arctica), kittiwakes (Rissa tridactyla), and common eiders (Somateria mollissima). These birds can often be seen nesting on the cliffs and foraging along the coastline.

- During a boat tour, I was delighted to see a colony of puffins nesting on a rocky island. Their distinctive colorful beaks and comical waddling made them a joy to watch. The sight of these charismatic birds, along with the calls of the kittiwakes, added to the enchantment of the fjords.

• **Raptors**:

- **Description**: Raptors, such as the white-tailed eagle (Haliaeetus albicilla), are commonly spotted in the fjords. These majestic birds of prey are known for their impressive wingspan and keen hunting skills.

- One afternoon, while hiking near a fjord, I was fortunate to witness a white-tailed eagle soaring high above. Its powerful wings and sharp talons were a testament to its prowess as a hunter. Watching it glide effortlessly through the sky was a humbling experience.

3. Terrestrial Animals:
• **Mammals**:

- **Description**: The forests and valleys of the fjords are home to a variety of mammals, including red deer (Cervus elaphus), moose (Alces alces), and red foxes (Vulpes vulpes). These animals are well-adapted to the diverse habitats of the fjords.

- During a quiet morning hike, I spotted a group of red deer grazing in a meadow. Their graceful movements and alert demeanor were captivating. Another time, I encountered a red fox trotting along a forest trail, its bright coat standing out against the greenery. These encounters with wildlife added a sense of wonder to my fjord explorations.

• **Amphibians and Reptiles**:

- **Description**: While less common, amphibians and reptiles, such as the common frog (Rana temporaria) and the viviparous lizard (Zootoca vivipara), can also be found in the fjords' diverse habitats.

- On a damp, rainy day, I came across a small pond filled with croaking frogs. Their calls created a symphony of sounds, and I watched as they hopped from one lily pad to another. It was a reminder of the intricate web of life that thrives in the fjords.

The flora and fauna of the Norwegian fjords are a testament to the incredible biodiversity and resilience of nature. From the hardy alpine plants and towering coniferous forests to the majestic whales, playful puffins, and graceful deer, the fjords are a haven for a wide variety of species. Exploring this rich tapestry of life adds depth and meaning to the fjord cruise experience, allowing you to connect with the natural world in a profound and unforgettable way.

Whale Watching and Marine Lifej

The Norwegian fjords are a haven for marine life, offering incredible opportunities for whale watching and observing diverse marine species in their natural habitat. The deep, nutrient-rich waters of the fjords attract a variety of marine

mammals and other sea creatures, making it a must-visit destination for nature enthusiasts and wildlife lovers. Let's dive into the world of whale watching and marine life in the fjords, enriched with personal experiences and observations.

Whale Watching

1. Orcas (Killer Whales)
• **Description**: Orcas, also known as killer whales, are one of the most iconic marine mammals found in the Norwegian fjords. These magnificent creatures are known for their striking black and white coloration and their highly social behavior.
• **Best Time to See**: Orcas are most commonly spotted in the winter months, from October to January, when they follow the herring migration into the fjords.
• One of the most thrilling moments of my fjord cruise was spotting a pod of orcas gliding gracefully through the water. Their synchronized movements and playful behavior were mesmerizing to watch. The sight of these powerful and intelligent animals in their natural environment was a truly unforgettable experience.

2. Humpback Whales
• **Description**: Humpback whales are known for their acrobatic displays and distinctive tail flukes. These gentle giants migrate to the Norwegian fjords to feed on the abundant herring and other fish.
• **Best Time to See**: Humpback whales are often seen from November to January, during their feeding season in the fjords.
• Watching a humpback whale breach the surface and splash back into the water was a

breathtaking sight. The sheer size and grace of these whales left me in awe. It was a privilege to witness their behavior up close, and the experience deepened my appreciation for the marine ecosystem.

3. Minke Whales

• **Description**: Minke whales are smaller baleen whales commonly found in the fjords. They are known for their curious nature and can often be seen approaching boats.

• **Best Time to See**: Minke whales can be spotted throughout the year, but sightings are more frequent during the summer months.

• During a fjord safari, I had the opportunity to see a minke whale surface nearby. Its sleek, dark body and the characteristic blow were fascinating to observe. The whale's curiosity brought it close to our boat, providing an intimate and unforgettable encounter.

4. Harbour Porpoises

• **Description**: Harbour porpoises are small, shy cetaceans that can be seen in the fjords. They are known for their fast swimming and preference for shallow coastal waters.

• **Best Time to See**: Harbour porpoises can be seen year-round, often in the quieter, more sheltered areas of the fjords.

• Spotting a group of harbour porpoises was a delightful experience. Their quick, darting movements and occasional leaps out of the water added an element of excitement to the boat tour. Though more elusive than other cetaceans, seeing them was a special treat.

Other Marine Life

1. Seals

• **Description**: The fjords are home to several species of seals, including the common seal (harbour seal) and the grey seal. These playful mammals are often seen lounging on rocks or swimming near the shoreline.

• I remember watching a group of seals basking on the rocks, their sleek bodies glistening in the sunlight. Occasionally, they would slip into the water and swim gracefully, their heads popping up curiously to observe us. Their playful antics and expressive faces made them a joy to watch.

2. Seabirds

• **Description**: The fjords are a paradise for birdwatchers, with a rich diversity of seabirds, including puffins, kittiwakes, and guillemots. These birds can be seen nesting on the cliffs and foraging along the coastline.

• Seeing a colony of puffins on a rocky island was a highlight of my trip. Their colorful beaks and endearing behavior made them a favorite among the passengers. The sight of seabirds soaring gracefully over the water and diving for fish added to the enchantment of the fjords.

3. Fish and Invertebrates

• **Description**: The waters of the fjords are teeming with fish and invertebrates, including cod, herring, mackerel, crabs, and shrimp. These species play a crucial role in the fjord's ecosystem and support a variety of marine predators.

• While kayaking in the fjords, I marveled at the clarity of the water, which allowed me to see schools of fish swimming below. The diversity of marine life was astounding, and I felt a deep appreciation for the richness of the fjord's underwater world.

Conservation and Responsible Whale Watching

Conservation Efforts
• The Norwegian fjords are part of a protected marine environment, with efforts in place to conserve and protect the diverse marine life. Responsible tourism and sustainable practices are encouraged to ensure the long-term health of the ecosystem.

Responsible Whale Watching
• Whale watching tours in the fjords follow strict guidelines to minimize disturbance to the animals. Boats maintain a respectful distance, avoid chasing or cornering the whales, and operate at slow speeds to reduce noise and impact.

Participating in a responsible whale watching tour was a rewarding experience. The knowledgeable guides shared insights about the behavior and conservation of the whales, enhancing our understanding and appreciation. The emphasis on respectful observation allowed us to enjoy the encounters while minimizing our impact on the marine environment.

Whale watching and observing marine life in the Norwegian fjords is an awe-inspiring experience that connects you with the beauty and diversity of the natural world. The opportunity to see majestic whales, playful seals, and a variety of seabirds in their natural habitat is a highlight of any fjord cruise. By supporting responsible tourism and conservation efforts, we can help protect these incredible species and their environment for future generations to enjoy.

Bird Watching and Wildlife Photography Tips

The Norwegian fjords are a paradise for bird watchers and wildlife photographers, offering stunning landscapes and diverse ecosystems that attract a wide variety of bird species and other wildlife. Capturing the beauty of these creatures in their natural habitat requires patience, skill, and a bit of planning. Let me share some tips and insights on bird watching and wildlife photography in the fjords, enriched with personal experiences and observations.

Bird Watching in the Norwegian Fjords

Best Bird Watching Spots:
• **Coastal Cliffs and Islands**: The rugged coastal cliffs and islands are home to numerous seabird colonies. Puffins, kittiwakes, guillemots, and razorbills can be seen nesting and foraging in these areas.
• **Wetlands and Estuaries**: These areas attract wading birds and waterfowl, including herons, ducks, and geese. The diverse habitats provide ample opportunities for spotting a variety of species.
• **Forested Areas**: The coniferous and deciduous forests are home to songbirds, woodpeckers, and raptors. Exploring these areas can reveal a wealth of bird life.

• One of the most memorable bird watching experiences I had was visiting a puffin colony on a remote island. Watching these charismatic birds with their colorful beaks and endearing behavior was a true delight. The sight of puffins flying to and from their burrows, often with a beak full of fish, was captivating.

Bird Watching Tips:

1. **Binoculars**: A good pair of binoculars is essential for bird watching. They allow you to observe birds up close without disturbing them. Look for binoculars with a magnification of at least 8x.

2. **Field Guide**: Carry a field guide specific to Norwegian birds. It will help you identify species and learn about their habits and habitats.

3. **Quiet and Patience**: Approach bird watching areas quietly and patiently. Sudden movements or loud noises can startle birds and cause them to flee.

4. **Early Morning and Late Afternoon**: Birds are most active during the early morning and late afternoon. Plan your bird watching excursions during these times for the best chances of spotting a variety of species.

Wildlife Photography Tips

Equipment:

1. **Camera and Lenses**: A DSLR or mirrorless camera with a good zoom lens (at least 200mm) is ideal for wildlife photography. A telephoto lens allows you to capture detailed shots of birds and other wildlife from a distance.

2. **Tripod**: A sturdy tripod helps stabilize your camera, especially when using long lenses. It ensures sharp images and allows for steady composition.

3. Extra Batteries and Memory Cards: Wildlife photography often involves long hours in the field. Carry extra batteries and memory cards to avoid running out of power or storage space.

• Capturing the graceful flight of a white-tailed eagle was a highlight of my wildlife photography journey. Using a telephoto lens, I was able to zoom in on the eagle as it soared high above the fjord. The challenge of tracking its movements and composing the shot was exhilarating, and the resulting image was a testament to the beauty and power of this magnificent bird.

Photography Tips:

1. **Know Your Subject**: Research the behavior and habits of the wildlife you plan to photograph. Understanding their patterns will help you anticipate their movements and capture better shots.

2. **Use Natural Light**: Natural light enhances the beauty of wildlife photos. Early morning and late afternoon provide soft, golden light that adds warmth and depth to your images.

3. **Composition**: Pay attention to composition. Use the rule of thirds to place your subject off-center and create a more dynamic image. Include elements of the natural habitat to provide context.

4. **Patience and Persistence**: Wildlife photography requires patience and persistence. Spend time observing and waiting for the perfect moment. Sometimes, the best shots come from simply being in the right place at the right time.

5. Ethical Practices: Always prioritize the well-being of the wildlife. Avoid disturbing animals or altering their natural behavior for the sake of a photograph. Practice ethical wildlife photography by maintaining a respectful distance and minimizing your impact on the environment.

Bird watching and wildlife photography in the Norwegian fjords offer unparalleled opportunities to connect with nature and capture the beauty of its inhabitants. Whether you're observing puffins nesting on coastal cliffs, photographing eagles soaring above the fjords, or simply enjoying the serene landscapes, the experience is both rewarding and inspiring. By following these tips and practicing patience and respect, you'll be able to create stunning images and unforgettable memories.

Chapter 7. Outdoor Adventures

Outdoor Adventures in the Norwegian Fjords

The Norwegian fjords are a paradise for outdoor enthusiasts, offering a wide range of activities that allow you to immerse yourself in the stunning landscapes and connect with nature. From hiking and trekking through scenic trails to kayaking on pristine waters and exploring majestic glaciers, the fjords offer something for every adventurer. Let's delve into the details of each of these activities, enriched with personal experiences and observations.

Hiking and Trekking in the Fjords

1. Popular Hiking Trails:
• **Besseggen Ridge**: One of Norway's most famous hikes, Besseggen Ridge offers breathtaking views of the turquoise waters of Gjende Lake and the surrounding mountains. The challenging trail covers approximately 14 kilometers and takes around 6-8 hours to complete.

   - Hiking Besseggen Ridge was an exhilarating adventure. The ascent was steep and demanding, but the reward was the awe-inspiring panorama of Gjende Lake and the rugged peaks. The sense of accomplishment upon reaching the summit was unmatched, and the views were simply unforgettable.
• **Romsdalseggen Ridge**: This dramatic ridge hike offers stunning vistas of the Romsdal Alps, the fjord, and the valley below. The trail is approximately 10 kilometers long and takes around 6-7 hours to complete.

   - Romsdalseggen Ridge provided some of the most spectacular scenery I've ever encountered. The sheer cliffs and jagged peaks created a dramatic backdrop, and the sense of being on top of the world was incredibly fulfilling. The hike was challenging but immensely rewarding.
• Preikestolen (Pulpit Rock): This iconic hike leads to a flat-topped cliff that juts out 604 meters above the Lysefjord. The 8-kilometer round trip takes around 4-5 hours to complete and offers breathtaking views of the fjord.

   - The hike to Preikestolen was a highlight of my fjord adventure. The well-marked trail took us through diverse landscapes, from dense forests to rocky terrain. Standing on the edge of Pulpit Rock, with the fjord stretching out below, was an awe-inspiring moment that left me speechless.

2. Hiking Tips:
• **Proper Gear**: Wear sturdy hiking boots with good ankle support. Dress in layers to accommodate changing weather conditions and bring a waterproof jacket.
• **Safety First**: Check the weather forecast before heading out and be prepared for sudden changes. Carry a map, compass, and sufficient water and snacks. Always hike with a buddy or inform someone of your plans.
• **Respect Nature**: Stay on marked trails to protect the fragile vegetation. Leave no trace

by packing out all trash and respecting wildlife.

Kayaking and Paddleboarding

1. Kayaking Adventures:
• Why Kayak in the Fjords: Kayaking allows you to explore the fjords from a unique perspective, gliding through the calm waters surrounded by towering cliffs and lush greenery. It's a peaceful and immersive way to connect with nature.
• Popular Kayaking Spots: Aurlandsfjord, Nærøyfjord, and Geirangerfjord are popular kayaking destinations, offering stunning scenery and opportunities to spot marine life.
   - Kayaking in Nærøyfjord was a serene and unforgettable experience. The fjord's narrow passage created a sense of intimacy with the landscape, and the silence was broken only by the sound of my paddle slicing through the water. I spotted seals sunbathing on the rocks and eagles soaring overhead, making it a truly magical adventure.

2. Paddleboarding:
• Why Paddleboard in the Fjords: Paddleboarding offers a fun and exciting way to explore the fjords, providing a full-body workout and the thrill of balancing on the water. It's a great option for those looking for a different kind of water adventure.
• Popular Paddleboarding Spots: Many of the same fjords that are popular for kayaking also offer excellent paddleboarding opportunities.
   - Paddleboarding on Aurlandsfjord was both challenging and exhilarating. The feeling of gliding across the water while surrounded by breathtaking scenery was incredibly rewarding. It required focus and balance, but the sense of achievement made it all worthwhile.

3. Tips for Kayaking and Paddleboarding:
• Safety Gear: Always wear a life jacket and consider using a wetsuit for added warmth and buoyancy. Carry a dry bag for your valuables and essentials.
• Weather Awareness: Check the weather forecast and be mindful of changing conditions. Avoid kayaking or paddleboarding in rough waters or strong winds.
• Respect Marine Life: Maintain a respectful distance from wildlife and avoid disturbing their natural behavior. Practice responsible tourism by minimizing your impact on the environment.

Glacier Exploration and Ice Climbing

1. Glacier Hiking:
• **Why Explore Glaciers**: Glacier hiking offers a unique opportunity to explore the ancient ice formations and witness the raw power of nature. It's an adventurous activity that takes you into the heart of the frozen wilderness.
• **Popular Glaciers**: Briksdal Glacier, Nigardsbreen Glacier, and Folgefonna Glacier are among the most popular glaciers for hiking in the fjords.
   - Hiking on the Briksdal Glacier was an awe-inspiring experience. Equipped with crampons and an ice axe, we trekked across the shimmering blue ice, marveling at the crevasses and ice formations. The guide's

knowledge about the glacier's history and geology added depth to the adventure.

2. Ice Climbing:

• **Why Ice Climb in the Fjords**: Ice climbing offers an adrenaline-pumping challenge, allowing you to scale vertical ice walls and frozen waterfalls. It's an activity that tests both physical strength and mental determination.

• **Popular Ice Climbing Spots**: The fjords offer several ice climbing opportunities, with guides and instructors available to ensure a safe and rewarding experience.

   - Ice climbing on the Nigardsbreen Glacier was an exhilarating and demanding adventure. The thrill of ascending the ice wall, using ice axes and crampons, was unmatched. The sense of accomplishment upon reaching the top was immense, and the views from the glacier were breathtaking.

3. Tips for Glacier Hiking and Ice Climbing:

• **Proper Equipment**: Use specialized equipment, including crampons, ice axes, and helmets. Wear layered clothing to stay warm and dry.

• **Guided Tours**: Always join a guided tour led by experienced guides. They provide essential safety training and equipment, as well as insights into the glacier's history and geology.

• **Physical Fitness**: Ensure you are in good physical condition, as glacier hiking and ice climbing can be physically demanding. Training and preparation are key to a successful and enjoyable experience.

The Norwegian fjords offer a wealth of outdoor adventures, from hiking and trekking through scenic trails to kayaking on pristine waters and exploring majestic glaciers. Each activity provides a unique way to connect with the stunning landscapes and immerse yourself in the natural beauty of the fjords. Whether you're seeking the thrill of ice climbing or the serenity of kayaking, there's something for every adventurer to enjoy.

Fishing and Angling

Fishing and angling in the Norwegian fjords offer a serene and rewarding way to connect with nature and experience the region's rich aquatic life. The fjords are renowned for their pristine waters, abundant fish species, and breathtaking landscapes, making them a perfect destination for both novice and experienced anglers. Let's delve into the details of fishing and angling in the fjords, enriched with personal experiences and observations.

Why Fish in the Fjords

Rich Biodiversity:

• The fjords are home to a diverse array of fish species, including cod, haddock, mackerel, herring, and salmon. The nutrient-rich waters provide an ideal habitat for these species, making the fjords a prime fishing destination.

Stunning Scenery:

• Fishing in the fjords allows you to immerse yourself in some of the most beautiful landscapes in the world. The backdrop of towering cliffs, lush greenery, and tranquil waters creates a serene and picturesque setting for your fishing adventures.

Cultural Tradition:

• Fishing is an integral part of Norway's cultural heritage, and many local communities have a deep connection to the sea. By participating in fishing activities, you can gain insights into the traditional practices and customs that have been passed down through generations.

Types of Fishing

1. Sea Fishing:
• Description: Sea fishing in the fjords involves fishing from a boat or the shoreline. The deep fjord waters are ideal for catching a variety of fish species, including cod, pollock, and haddock.
• One of my most memorable experiences was joining a local fishing tour in the fjords. The guide took us to some of the best fishing spots, where we cast our lines into the deep waters. The excitement of feeling a tug on the line and reeling in a sizeable cod was exhilarating. The stunning views of the fjord added to the magic of the experience.

2. Fly Fishing:
• Description: Fly fishing is a popular method for catching salmon and trout in the rivers and streams that flow into the fjords. This technique involves using a lightweight fly rod and an artificial fly to mimic the appearance of insects.
• Fly fishing in a pristine river surrounded by lush forests was a deeply meditative experience. The rhythmic casting of the fly rod and the anticipation of a trout rising to take the fly created a sense of harmony with nature. The thrill of landing a beautiful salmon was an unforgettable highlight.

3. Ice Fishing:
• Description: Ice fishing is a unique winter activity that involves fishing through a hole drilled in the ice. It's a popular way to catch species like Arctic char and trout.
• Ice fishing on a frozen fjord was a fascinating adventure. Equipped with an ice auger and a small fishing rod, we drilled holes in the ice and patiently waited for a bite. The stillness of the winter landscape and the camaraderie of fellow anglers made it a memorable and enjoyable experience.

Fishing Tips

1. Equipment:
• Proper Gear: Use appropriate fishing gear for the type of fishing you plan to do. This includes rods, reels, lines, hooks, and bait. For sea fishing, heavier tackle is recommended, while fly fishing requires specialized fly rods and flies.
• Clothing: Dress in layers and wear waterproof clothing to stay warm and dry. Good quality waders are essential for fly fishing in rivers and streams.

2. Local Knowledge:
• Guided Tours: Consider joining a guided fishing tour led by local experts. They can provide valuable insights into the best fishing spots, techniques, and local regulations.
• Fishing Licenses: Ensure you have the necessary fishing licenses and permits. Regulations vary depending on the location and type of fishing, so it's important to check with local authorities.

3. Respect Nature:

• Catch and Release: Practice catch and release to help preserve fish populations and maintain the ecological balance of the fjords. Use barbless hooks and handle fish gently to minimize stress and injury.

• Leave No Trace: Keep the fishing areas clean by packing out all trash and avoiding any damage to the natural environment.

Culinary Delights

1. Cooking Your Catch:

• **Description**: One of the joys of fishing in the fjords is the opportunity to cook and enjoy your fresh catch. Local restaurants and accommodations often provide facilities for guests to prepare their fish.

• After a successful day of sea fishing, we brought our catch back to the lodge, where the chef prepared a delicious meal. The fresh cod, grilled to perfection and served with local vegetables and a creamy sauce, was a culinary delight. Sharing the meal with fellow anglers while recounting the day's adventures was a perfect way to end the day.

2. Local Seafood:

• **Description**: If you prefer not to cook, you can still enjoy the bountiful seafood of the fjords at local restaurants. From smoked salmon and pickled herring to king crab and shrimp, the culinary offerings are diverse and delectable.

• Dining at a waterfront restaurant in a small fjord village, I savored a platter of assorted seafood, including shrimp, mussels, and crab. The flavors were exquisite, and the fresh, briny taste of the seafood was a testament to the fjord's rich marine life. The setting, with the gentle lapping of the waves and the backdrop of the fjord, made it an unforgettable dining experience.

Fishing and angling in the Norwegian fjords offer a serene and rewarding way to connect with nature and experience the region's rich aquatic life. Whether you're casting a line into the deep fjord waters, fly fishing in a tranquil river, or trying your hand at ice fishing, the experience is both thrilling and enriching. The opportunity to cook and savor your fresh catch, surrounded by the stunning landscapes of the fjords, adds an extra layer of enjoyment to the adventure.

Chapter 8. Cultural Experiences

Norwegian Heritage and Traditions

Norway's rich heritage and traditions are deeply rooted in its history, culture, and natural landscapes. The country's customs, folklore, and way of life have been shaped by centuries of seafaring, farming, and a close connection to nature. Exploring Norwegian heritage and traditions offers a fascinating glimpse into the heart and soul of this beautiful country. Let's delve into the key aspects of Norwegian heritage, enriched with personal experiences and observations.

Viking Heritage

1. Viking History:
• **Description**: The Vikings were seafaring Norse people who lived between the 8th and 11th centuries. They were known for their explorations, trade, and conquests. Norway was a central hub of Viking activity, and their legacy is still evident in the country's culture and traditions.
• Visiting the Viking Ship Museum in Oslo was a captivating journey into the past. The well-preserved Viking ships, burial artifacts, and detailed exhibits provided a fascinating insight into the lives of these legendary seafarers. Standing before the majestic Oseberg ship, I could almost imagine the Vikings setting sail on their epic voyages.

2. Viking Traditions:

• **Description**: Many modern Norwegian customs have their roots in Viking traditions. These include storytelling, folk music, and various festivals that celebrate Norse mythology and heritage.
• Attending a Viking reenactment festival was a unique and immersive experience. The festival featured traditional Viking games, music, and crafts. Watching the skilled reenactors demonstrate Viking combat techniques and hearing the enchanting sounds of the lyre and horn transported me back in time.

Folk Traditions and Festivals

1. Bunad (Traditional Costume):
• **Description**: The bunad is a traditional Norwegian costume worn during special occasions and celebrations. Each region has its own distinct style, featuring intricate embroidery, patterns, and colors.
• During Norway's Constitution Day (17th of May) celebrations, I witnessed the vibrant display of bunads worn by people of all ages. The streets were filled with the joyous sounds of parades, music, and laughter. The pride and cultural significance of the bunad were evident in the meticulous craftsmanship and the way people wore them with honor and respect.

2. Folk Music and Dance:

• **Description**: Norwegian folk music and dance are integral parts of the country's cultural heritage. Traditional instruments like the Hardanger fiddle (Hardingfele) and the langeleik are used to play lively tunes, often accompanied by traditional dances like the halling and springar.

• At a rural festival, I had the pleasure of watching a folk dance performance. The dancers, dressed in colorful costumes, moved gracefully to the lively tunes of the Hardanger fiddle. The energy and rhythm of the dance were infectious, and I found myself tapping my feet along with the beat. The sense of community and celebration was palpable.

3. Festivals and Celebrations:

• **Description**: Norway hosts a variety of festivals and celebrations throughout the year, many of which are steeped in tradition. These include the midsummer celebration (Jonsok), Christmas (Jul), and the Sami National Day.

• Celebrating Christmas in Norway was a heartwarming experience. The festive decorations, the scent of freshly baked cookies, and the tradition of lighting Advent candles created a cozy and joyous atmosphere. Attending a Christmas market, with its stalls offering handmade crafts and delicious treats, added to the festive spirit.

Sami Culture

1. Sami People:

• **Description**: The Sami are the indigenous people of northern Norway, Sweden, Finland, and the Kola Peninsula of Russia. They have a rich cultural heritage, including unique traditions, language, and reindeer herding.

• Visiting a Sami village in northern Norway was a profound experience. The Sami hosts warmly welcomed us and shared insights into their way of life. We learned about reindeer herding, listened to traditional joik (Sami chanting), and enjoyed a meal of bidos (reindeer stew) around an open fire. The deep connection between the Sami people and their land was evident in every aspect of their culture.

2. Sami Traditions:

• **Description**: Sami traditions include reindeer herding, traditional clothing (gákti), handicrafts (duodji), and storytelling. The annual reindeer migration and the celebration of the Sami National Day (February 6th) are significant events in Sami culture.

• Attending the Sami National Day celebrations was a colorful and vibrant experience. The streets were filled with Sami people dressed in their traditional gákti, proudly displaying their cultural identity. The festivities included music, dance, and storytelling, creating a sense of unity and pride in their heritage.

Norwegian Folklore

1. Myths and Legends:

• **Description**: Norwegian folklore is rich with myths and legends, featuring creatures like trolls, huldra, and nisse. These stories have been passed down through generations and continue to be a significant part of Norwegian cultural identity.

• Exploring the forests and mountains of Norway, I couldn't help but be reminded of the folklore that describes these landscapes as the homes of mythical creatures. The tales of trolls hiding in the shadows of the mountains added an element of enchantment to the already magical scenery. Visiting the Trollstigen (Troll's Path) and seeing the giant troll statues brought these legends to life.

2. Storytelling and Literature:
• **Description**: Storytelling is an important tradition in Norway, with a rich oral heritage that includes fairy tales, sagas, and epic poems. Norwegian literature, such as the works of Henrik Ibsen and Sigrid Undset, has also made significant contributions to world literature.
• Attending a storytelling session at a local cultural center was a captivating experience. The storyteller's expressive voice and vivid descriptions brought the tales to life, transporting the audience to a world of fantasy and adventure. The power of these stories to evoke emotions and create a sense of connection was truly remarkable.

Norwegian heritage and traditions are a rich tapestry of history, culture, and folklore that continue to shape the country's identity. From the legacy of the Vikings and the vibrant folk traditions to the unique Sami culture and the enchanting world of folklore, Norway's heritage is a source of pride and inspiration for its people. Exploring these traditions offers a deeper understanding of the country's soul and a meaningful connection to its past and present.

Visiting Historic Sites and Museums

Exploring historic sites and museums in Norway offers a fascinating journey through the country's rich history, culture, and heritage. From ancient Viking sites to modern art museums, Norway's diverse attractions provide a deep understanding of its past and present. Let's delve into some of the most notable historic sites and museums you should consider visiting, enriched with personal experiences and observations.

1. Viking Ship Museum (Vikingskipshuset) – Oslo

Description:
• The Viking Ship Museum in Oslo houses some of the world's best-preserved Viking ships and artifacts. The centerpiece of the museum is the Oseberg ship, a stunningly preserved Viking burial ship dating back to the 9th century. The museum also features the Gokstad and Tune ships, along with a variety of artifacts, including burial goods, tools, and textiles.

• Visiting the Viking Ship Museum was like stepping back in time. The sheer size and craftsmanship of the Viking ships were awe-inspiring. The detailed exhibits provided a glimpse into the lives of the Vikings, their seafaring skills, and their burial practices. Standing before the Oseberg ship, I felt a profound connection to Norway's Viking heritage.

2. Nidaros Cathedral (Nidarosdomen) – Trondheim

Description:

• Nidaros Cathedral is the largest medieval church in Scandinavia and one of Norway's most important religious and historic sites. Built over the tomb of St. Olav, the patron saint of Norway, the cathedral is a masterpiece of Gothic architecture with intricate sculptures, stunning stained glass windows, and a rich history.

• Walking into Nidaros Cathedral was a breathtaking experience. The grandeur of the architecture, the play of light through the stained glass windows, and the serene atmosphere created a sense of awe and reverence. Climbing the tower to get a panoramic view of Trondheim was an unforgettable highlight.

3. Bryggen (The Hanseatic Wharf) – Bergen

Description:
• Bryggen, a UNESCO World Heritage site, is a historic district in Bergen known for its colorful wooden buildings that date back to the Hanseatic period. The area is a testament to Bergen's history as a major trading hub and offers a glimpse into the lives of the merchants who once lived and worked there.

• Strolling through the narrow alleyways of Bryggen felt like wandering through history. The well-preserved buildings, with their charming facades and historic interiors, transported me to a bygone era. Visiting the Hanseatic Museum provided deeper insights into the daily lives and trade practices of the Hanseatic merchants.

4. Akershus Fortress (Akershus Festning) – Oslo

Description:
• Akershus Fortress is a medieval castle and fortress located in the heart of Oslo. Built in the late 13th century, it has served as a royal residence, military base, and prison. Today, it houses the Norwegian Armed Forces Museum and the Resistance Museum, which offer comprehensive exhibits on Norway's military history and World War II resistance efforts.

• Exploring Akershus Fortress was a fascinating journey through Norway's military history. The fortress's robust architecture and strategic location overlooking the Oslofjord provided a sense of its historical significance. The Resistance Museum's exhibits on Norway's resistance movement during World War II were particularly moving and inspiring.

5. Kon-Tiki Museum – Oslo

Description:
• The Kon-Tiki Museum is dedicated to the adventures of the Norwegian explorer Thor Heyerdahl. It showcases the original Kon-Tiki raft, which Heyerdahl used to sail from Peru to Polynesia in 1947, along with artifacts from his other expeditions and documentaries about his explorations.

• Visiting the Kon-Tiki Museum was an adventure in itself. The story of Thor Heyerdahl's daring voyages and his determination to prove his theories about ancient seafaring routes were incredibly inspiring. Seeing the original Kon-Tiki raft up close and learning about the challenges of the expedition gave me a deep appreciation for Heyerdahl's pioneering spirit.

6. Fram Museum – Oslo

Description:
• The Fram Museum is dedicated to the exploration of the polar regions. It houses the Fram, the wooden ship used by Norwegian explorers Fridtjof Nansen, Otto Sverdrup, and Roald Amundsen for their Arctic and Antarctic expeditions. The museum offers exhibits on polar exploration, including artifacts, photographs, and interactive displays.

• Stepping aboard the Fram was like embarking on a polar expedition. The well-preserved ship and the detailed exhibits provided a vivid portrayal of the challenges and triumphs of polar exploration. Learning about the courage and ingenuity of Nansen, Sverdrup, and Amundsen left me with a sense of admiration for these pioneering explorers.

7. The Norwegian Folk Museum (Norsk Folkemuseum) – Oslo

Description:
• The Norwegian Folk Museum is an open-air museum showcasing traditional Norwegian culture and heritage. It features over 150 historic buildings, including farmhouses, stave churches, and urban dwellings, as well as exhibits on folk art, clothing, and daily life.

• Wandering through the Norwegian Folk Museum felt like stepping into a living history book. The meticulously reconstructed buildings and the interactive exhibits brought Norway's past to life. I particularly enjoyed exploring the Gol Stave Church, a beautifully preserved medieval church with intricate wood carvings.

8. Røros Mining Town – Røros

Description:
• Røros is a UNESCO World Heritage site known for its well-preserved wooden buildings and its history as a mining town. Founded in the 17th century, Røros was a major center for copper mining. Today, it offers a glimpse into the lives of the miners and the town's unique architectural heritage.

• Visiting Røros was like stepping back in time. The charming wooden buildings, cobblestone streets, and historic mining structures created a picturesque and immersive experience. The Røros Museum provided fascinating insights into the town's mining history and the daily lives of its inhabitants.

9. Lofoten Viking Museum (Lofotr Vikingmuseum) – Lofoten Islands

Description:
• The Lofoten Viking Museum is located in Borg, a significant Viking archaeological site in the Lofoten Islands. The museum features a reconstructed Viking longhouse, as well as artifacts and exhibits that provide a comprehensive overview of Viking life and culture.

• Exploring the Lofoten Viking Museum was a captivating journey into the world of the Vikings. The reconstructed longhouse, with its detailed interiors and interactive exhibits, allowed me to experience Viking life firsthand.

Participating in Viking activities, such as axe throwing and traditional crafts, added an element of fun and engagement.

Visiting historic sites and museums in Norway offers a rich and immersive experience, providing deep insights into the country's history, culture, and heritage. From Viking ships and medieval cathedrals to open-air museums and mining towns, each site tells a unique story that adds to the tapestry of Norway's past and present. Exploring these attractions allows you to connect with Norway's heritage in a meaningful and memorable way.

Traditional Music and Dance

Norwegian traditional music and dance are integral parts of the country's cultural heritage, reflecting its history, folklore, and deep connection to nature. From haunting melodies played on ancient instruments to lively dances performed at festivals and celebrations, Norway's musical and dance traditions offer a rich and vibrant tapestry of cultural expression. Let's explore some of the key elements of traditional Norwegian music and dance, enriched with personal experiences and observations.

1. Hardanger Fiddle (Hardingfele)

Description:
• The Hardanger fiddle, known as the Hardingfele, is a traditional Norwegian string instrument similar to a violin but with a unique construction and sound. It has an additional set of sympathetic strings that resonate with the main strings, creating a rich and complex tone. The fiddle is often intricately decorated with inlays and carvings.

Role in Traditional Music:
• The Hardanger fiddle is central to Norwegian folk music and is commonly used to play traditional tunes called "slåtter." These tunes are often associated with specific dances and occasions, such as weddings and festivals.

• Listening to a skilled Hardanger fiddle player was a mesmerizing experience. The music had a haunting and ethereal quality that seemed to evoke the landscapes of Norway. The intricate ornamentation of the fiddle and the complex rhythms of the slåtter added depth and beauty to the performance.

2. Langeleik

Description:
• The langeleik is a traditional Norwegian zither-like instrument with a long, narrow body and a varying number of strings. It is played by plucking or strumming the strings while pressing down on the frets to create different notes.

Role in Traditional Music:
• The langeleik is often used to accompany singing and dancing. Its simple yet melodic sound provides a gentle and soothing backdrop to folk songs and ballads.

• Hearing the gentle melodies of the langeleik at a local cultural event was a calming and meditative experience. The music had a timeless quality, and the sound of the plucked strings resonated beautifully in the natural surroundings.

3. Traditional Dance

1. Halling:
• **Description**: The halling is a traditional Norwegian folk dance characterized by its lively and acrobatic movements. Dancers perform impressive leaps, kicks, and spins, often incorporating elements of athleticism and strength.
• Watching a halling dance performance was exhilarating. The dancers, dressed in traditional costumes, displayed incredible agility and coordination. The energetic music and rhythmic clapping of the audience created a festive and dynamic atmosphere.

2. Springar:
• **Description**: The springar is a couple's dance that features a distinctive 3/4 time rhythm. It is often accompanied by the Hardanger fiddle and involves graceful movements and intricate footwork.
• Attending a springar dance at a rural festival was a delightful experience. The couples moved in perfect harmony, their movements flowing seamlessly with the rhythm of the fiddle. The dance's graceful and joyful nature was a testament to the deep cultural connection between the dancers and the music.

3. Rørospols:
• **Description**: The Rørospols is a traditional dance from the Røros region. It features a lively and spirited tempo, with dancers moving in circular patterns and performing intricate steps.

• Participating in a Rørospols dance workshop was both challenging and fun. The dance required quick footwork and coordination, but the instructors were patient and encouraging. The sense of camaraderie and shared joy among the participants made it a memorable experience.

4. Sami Music and Dance

1. Joik:
• **Description**: Joik is a traditional form of Sami singing that is characterized by its improvisational and personal nature. Each joik is often dedicated to a specific person, animal, or place and serves as a form of musical storytelling.
• Listening to a Sami joik was a deeply moving experience. The singer's voice conveyed a sense of connection and reverence for the subject of the joik. The haunting and melodic tones created an intimate and emotional atmosphere.

2. Sami Dance:
• **Description**: Sami dance traditions are often performed at cultural events and celebrations. They include a variety of group dances that emphasize community and togetherness.
• Witnessing a Sami dance performance during the Sami National Day celebrations was a vibrant and joyful experience. The dancers, dressed in traditional gákti, moved with energy and enthusiasm, celebrating their heritage and cultural identity.

5. Folk Songs and Ballads

Description:

• Norwegian folk songs and ballads are an essential part of the country's musical heritage. These songs often tell stories of love, nature, legends, and everyday life. They are typically passed down through generations and are performed at various cultural events and gatherings.

• Attending a folk singing session at a local inn was a heartwarming experience. The singer's voice, accompanied by the gentle strumming of the langeleik, filled the room with warmth and nostalgia. The audience joined in on familiar refrains, creating a sense of unity and shared tradition.

Traditional music and dance are vital components of Norway's cultural heritage, reflecting the country's history, folklore, and deep connection to nature. From the enchanting melodies of the Hardanger fiddle to the lively steps of the halling and the soulful tones of Sami joik, Norway's musical and dance traditions offer a rich and vibrant tapestry of cultural expression. Exploring these traditions provides a deeper understanding of Norway's cultural identity and a meaningful connection to its past and present.

Festivals and Events

Norway is a country rich in cultural traditions, and its festivals and events reflect this vibrant heritage. From national celebrations and music festivals to unique local traditions and cultural gatherings, Norway's festivals offer a glimpse into the heart and soul of the country. Let's explore some of the key festivals and events that you should experience, enriched with personal experiences and observations.

1. Constitution Day (Syttende Mai) – May 17th

Description:
• Constitution Day, known as Syttende Mai, is Norway's national day and one of the most important celebrations in the country. It commemorates the signing of the Norwegian Constitution on May 17, 1814. The day is marked by parades, traditional costumes, music, and festivities.

Highlights:
• **Parades**: Children and adults participate in parades, waving Norwegian flags and singing patriotic songs. The main parade in Oslo is especially grand, with the Royal Family greeting the crowd from the balcony of the Royal Palace.
• **Bunad**: Many Norwegians wear their traditional costumes, called bunads, which vary by region and are adorned with intricate embroidery and designs.
• **Festivities**: The day is filled with music, dancing, games, and delicious food, including hot dogs, ice cream, and traditional Norwegian dishes.

• Celebrating Constitution Day in Oslo was a joyous and festive experience. The streets were filled with people of all ages, proudly wearing their bunads and waving flags. The sense of national pride and unity was palpable, and the atmosphere was electric with music, laughter, and celebration. Joining the crowd in singing the national anthem and watching the

Royal Family wave from the palace balcony was a highlight of the day.

2. St. John's Eve (Jonsok or Sankthans) – June 23rd

Description:
• St. John's Eve, also known as Jonsok or Sankthans, is a traditional midsummer celebration that takes place on June 23rd. It is a time to celebrate the summer solstice with bonfires, music, dancing, and feasting.

Highlights:
• **Bonfires**: Large bonfires are lit along the coast and in communities across Norway, symbolizing the triumph of light over darkness.
• **Folk Music and Dance**: Traditional music and folk dances are performed, creating a lively and festive atmosphere.
• **Feasting**: Families and friends gather for outdoor picnics and barbecues, enjoying seasonal foods and drinks.

• Celebrating St. John's Eve in a small coastal village was a magical experience. As the sun began to set, the community gathered around a towering bonfire on the beach. The flickering flames and the sound of traditional music created a warm and enchanting atmosphere. We joined in the dancing and shared a delicious meal of grilled fish and fresh berries, celebrating the long days of summer.

3. Sami National Day – February 6th

Description:
• Sami National Day celebrates the culture and heritage of the Sami people, the indigenous people of northern Norway, Sweden, Finland, and Russia. The day is marked with cultural events, traditional music, dance, and ceremonies.

Highlights:
• **Gákti**: Sami people wear their traditional clothing, called gákti, which is colorful and intricately decorated.
• **Joik:** Traditional Sami singing, known as joik, is performed, often telling stories of people, animals, and landscapes.
• **Reindeer Racing**: In some Sami communities, reindeer races are held, showcasing the important role of reindeer in Sami culture.

• Attending the Sami National Day celebrations in Karasjok was a vibrant and enriching experience. The streets were filled with Sami people proudly wearing their gákti, and the air was filled with the sounds of joik and traditional music. Watching a reindeer race and participating in a Sami dance added to the excitement of the day. The warmth and hospitality of the Sami community made the celebration even more special.

4. Bergen International Festival (Festspillene i Bergen) – Late May to Early June

Description:
• The Bergen International Festival is one of Norway's premier arts festivals, featuring a diverse program of music, dance, theater, and visual arts. It attracts artists and performers from around the world and takes place in various venues across Bergen.

Highlights:

• **Concerts**: The festival features a wide range of musical performances, from classical and contemporary to folk and jazz.

• **Theater and Dance**: The program includes theatrical productions, dance performances, and multidisciplinary art shows.

• **Art Exhibitions**: Visual arts are showcased in galleries and public spaces, offering a platform for both established and emerging artists.

• Attending the Bergen International Festival was a cultural feast. The city came alive with artistic energy, and there was something for everyone to enjoy. I attended a stunning classical concert in the historic Grieg Hall, watched a contemporary dance performance in an intimate theater, and explored thought-provoking art installations in the city's galleries. The festival's eclectic program and vibrant atmosphere made it a highlight of my time in Bergen.

5. Peer Gynt Festival (Peer Gynt-stemnet) – Early August

Description:

• The Peer Gynt Festival, held in the Gudbrandsdalen region, celebrates Norway's literary heritage and the iconic play "Peer Gynt" by Henrik Ibsen. The festival features outdoor theater performances, music, and cultural events inspired by Ibsen's work.

Highlights:

• **Outdoor Theater**: The highlight of the festival is the outdoor production of "Peer Gynt," performed against the stunning backdrop of the Norwegian landscape.

• **Music and Dance**: The festival includes concerts, folk music, and dance performances, adding to the festive atmosphere.

• **Cultural Activities**: Workshops, lectures, and exhibitions provide insights into Ibsen's life and work.

• Watching the outdoor performance of "Peer Gynt" was a mesmerizing experience. The natural setting of Lake Gålåvatnet provided a breathtaking stage, and the actors' powerful performances brought Ibsen's characters to life. The combination of theater, music, and the beauty of the Norwegian countryside made the festival a truly immersive cultural experience.

6. Oslo Jazz Festival – Mid-August

Description:

• The Oslo Jazz Festival is a week-long celebration of jazz music, featuring performances by local and international artists. The festival takes place in various venues across Oslo, including concert halls, clubs, and outdoor stages.

Highlights:

• **Live Performances**: The festival offers a diverse lineup of jazz performances, from traditional and swing to modern and experimental jazz.

• **Workshops and Masterclasses**: Musicians and enthusiasts can participate in workshops and masterclasses led by renowned jazz artists.

• **Open-Air Concerts**: Outdoor concerts in parks and public spaces provide a relaxed and enjoyable way to experience the music.

• Attending the Oslo Jazz Festival was a musical delight. The city's venues were filled with the sounds of jazz, and each performance offered something unique. I enjoyed an intimate club performance by a talented Norwegian trio, danced to a lively swing band in an outdoor park, and learned new techniques in a jazz improvisation workshop. The festival's diverse program and the city's vibrant jazz scene made it an unforgettable experience.

7. Northern Lights Festival (Nordlysfestivalen) – Late January to Early February

Description:
• The Northern Lights Festival, held in Tromsø, celebrates classical and contemporary music against the backdrop of the Arctic winter. The festival features a range of musical performances, from orchestral and choral concerts to jazz and folk music.

Highlights:
• **Concerts**: The festival offers a diverse program of concerts, including performances by world-class musicians and local talent.
• **Northern Lights**: The festival coincides with the peak season for viewing the Northern Lights, providing a magical natural spectacle.
• **Cultural Events**: The festival includes art exhibitions, film screenings, and cultural activities that showcase the unique Arctic heritage of Tromsø.

• Attending the Northern Lights Festival in Tromsø was a magical experience. The combination of exquisite music and the chance to witness the Northern Lights made it truly special. One evening, after a captivating concert in the Arctic Cathedral, I stepped outside to see the sky illuminated by the shimmering aurora borealis. The beauty of the natural phenomenon, combined with the cultural richness of the festival, left me in awe.

8. Riddu Riđđu Festival – Mid-July

Description:
• The Riddu Riđđu Festival is an indigenous festival that celebrates Sami and other indigenous cultures from around the world. Held in the village of Manndalen in Northern Norway, the festival features music, dance, art, and cultural events.

Highlights:
• **Music and Dance**: The festival showcases performances by indigenous artists, including traditional Sami joik, drumming, and contemporary music.
• **Cultural Workshops**: Attendees can participate in workshops on traditional crafts, storytelling, and indigenous knowledge.
• Art Exhibitions: The festival includes exhibitions of indigenous art, providing a platform for artists to share their work.

• The Riddu Riđđu Festival was a vibrant and enlightening celebration of indigenous cultures. The music and dance performances were both powerful and captivating, and the workshops offered a hands-on experience of Sami traditions. The festival fostered a sense of unity and respect among attendees from diverse backgrounds, making it a truly enriching experience.

Chapter 9. Local Markets and Artisan Crafts

Exploring Local Markets

Norway's local markets offer a delightful glimpse into the country's culture, traditions, and culinary delights. These markets are vibrant hubs where locals and visitors alike can experience the flavors, crafts, and unique products that define Norwegian life. Let's explore some of the most notable local markets in Norway, enriched with personal experiences and observations.

1. Mathallen Food Hall – Oslo

Description:
• Mathallen Food Hall is a bustling indoor market located in the Vulkan area of Oslo. It features a wide variety of food stalls, restaurants, and specialty shops offering fresh produce, meats, seafood, cheeses, baked goods, and more. The market is a haven for food lovers and a great place to sample Norwegian and international cuisine.

Highlights:
• **Local Delicacies**: Sample traditional Norwegian foods such as reindeer sausages, smoked salmon, and brunost (brown cheese). Don't miss the fresh seafood, including oysters and shrimp.
• **Gourmet Products**: Discover artisanal cheeses, cured meats, and gourmet chocolates. The market also offers a selection of fine wines and craft beers.

• **Cooking Classes and Events**: Mathallen hosts cooking classes, food tastings, and culinary events, providing opportunities to learn from local chefs and food experts.

• Visiting Mathallen Food Hall was a culinary adventure. I spent hours wandering through the market, sampling delicious treats from various stalls. One of my favorite experiences was trying a traditional Norwegian open-faced sandwich topped with smoked salmon and a dollop of crème fraîche. The flavors were exquisite, and the bustling atmosphere of the market made it a lively and enjoyable visit.

2. Torvet – Trondheim

Description:
• Torvet is the central square in Trondheim and hosts a vibrant outdoor market. The market is known for its fresh produce, flowers, and local crafts. It's a popular gathering place for locals and visitors, offering a wide range of products and a lively atmosphere.

Highlights:
• **Fresh Produce**: Browse stalls selling fresh fruits, vegetables, berries, and herbs. The market is a great place to find seasonal produce and locally grown ingredients.
• **Local Crafts**: Discover handmade crafts, including traditional knitwear, ceramics, and

jewelry. The market is an excellent spot to find unique souvenirs and gifts.

• **Flowers and Plants**: Admire the colorful displays of flowers and plants, perfect for brightening up your home or as a thoughtful gift.

• Exploring Torvet was a delightful experience. The market was filled with the vibrant colors and scents of fresh produce and flowers. I enjoyed chatting with the friendly vendors and learning about their products. One stall offered a tasting of fresh strawberries, which were incredibly sweet and juicy. The market's lively atmosphere and the sense of community made it a memorable visit.

3. Fisketorget (Fish Market) – Bergen

Description:
• Fisketorget is Bergen's famous fish market, located in the heart of the city by the harbor. The market has been a hub of seafood trade for centuries and offers a wide variety of fresh fish, shellfish, and other seafood products. It's a must-visit destination for seafood lovers.

Highlights:
• **Fresh Seafood**: Browse an impressive selection of fresh fish, including cod, salmon, halibut, and mackerel. The market also offers shellfish such as shrimp, crab, and lobster.
• **Seafood Delicacies**: Sample traditional Norwegian seafood dishes, such as fiskekaker (fish cakes), gravlaks (cured salmon), and whale meat. Some stalls offer seafood platters that you can enjoy on the spot.
• **Local Specialties**: Discover regional specialties like lutefisk (dried cod soaked in lye) and rakfisk (fermented fish). These unique dishes provide a taste of Norway's culinary heritage.

• Visiting Fisketorget was a seafood lover's dream. The market was bustling with activity, and the displays of fresh seafood were a feast for the eyes. I couldn't resist trying a seafood platter, which included a variety of freshly caught fish and shellfish. The flavors were incredibly fresh and delicious, and the experience of dining by the harbor made it even more special.

4. Bondens Marked (Farmers' Market) – Various Locations

Description:
• Bondens Marked, or the Farmers' Market, is a network of markets held in various locations across Norway. These markets focus on locally produced, high-quality foods and crafts. They provide an opportunity for farmers and artisans to sell their products directly to consumers.

Highlights:
• **Seasonal Produce**: Find fresh fruits, vegetables, herbs, and berries, all locally grown and in season. The market is a great place to stock up on organic and sustainably sourced produce.
• **Artisanal Products**: Discover homemade jams, honey, cheeses, sausages, and baked goods. Many vendors offer samples, allowing you to taste before you buy.
• **Handmade Crafts**: Browse a selection of handmade crafts, including textiles, pottery, and wooden items. These unique products make excellent gifts and souvenirs.

• Attending a Bondens Marked in a small village was a heartwarming experience. The market was filled with an array of fresh produce and homemade goodies. I enjoyed sampling artisanal cheeses and chatting with the farmers about their products. One stall offered freshly baked bread, which was warm and crusty—perfect for pairing with local cheeses and jams. The market's friendly and welcoming atmosphere made it a delightful visit.

5. Christmas Markets – Various Locations

Description:
• Norway's Christmas markets are a magical experience, offering festive decorations, seasonal treats, and a warm holiday atmosphere. These markets are held in various towns and cities across the country during the Advent season.

Highlights:
• **Festive Decorations**: Wander through beautifully decorated stalls offering handmade ornaments, candles, and holiday decorations. The markets are adorned with twinkling lights and festive garlands.
• **Seasonal Treats**: Enjoy traditional Christmas treats such as pepperkaker (gingerbread cookies), gløgg (mulled wine), and krumkake (wafer cookies). Some markets also offer savory dishes like ribbe (roast pork) and pinnekjøtt (dried lamb ribs).
• **Gifts and Crafts**: Find unique gifts and crafts, including knitted sweaters, woolen mittens, and handcrafted jewelry. The markets offer a wide range of locally made products that capture the spirit of the season.

• Visiting a Christmas market in Oslo was a truly enchanting experience. The market was filled with the scent of gingerbread and mulled wine, and the stalls were brimming with festive decorations and gifts. I enjoyed sipping on hot gløgg while browsing the handmade crafts and listening to carolers sing traditional Christmas songs. The market's joyful and cozy atmosphere made it a perfect way to celebrate the holiday season.

6. Røros Market (Rørosmartnan) – Røros

Description:
• The Røros Market, or Rørosmartnan, is an annual winter market held in the historic town of Røros. The market dates back to the 17th century and celebrates the town's mining heritage and cultural traditions. It features traditional crafts, local foods, and a festive atmosphere.

Highlights:
• **Traditional Crafts**: Discover handmade crafts, including woolen garments, wooden items, and pottery. The market showcases the craftsmanship of local artisans.
• **Local Foods**: Sample traditional foods such as reindeer sausages, cured meats, and baked goods. The market also offers hot beverages to warm you up on cold winter days.
• **Cultural Events**: Enjoy cultural events such as folk music performances, horse-drawn sleigh rides, and historical reenactments. The market's lively atmosphere and rich traditions make it a unique experience.

• Attending the Røros Market was like stepping into a winter wonderland. The historic town was beautifully decorated, and the market stalls were filled with traditional crafts and delicious foods. I tried reindeer sausage for the first time, which was flavorful and hearty. The horse-drawn sleigh rides and folk music performances added to the festive atmosphere, making it a truly memorable visit.

Exploring local markets in Norway offers a delightful and immersive experience, providing insights into the country's culture, traditions, and culinary delights. From bustling food halls and outdoor farmers' markets to festive Christmas markets and historic winter fairs, each market offers a unique and vibrant atmosphere. Whether you're sampling fresh seafood at Fisketorget, browsing handmade crafts at Bondens Marked, or enjoying the festive spirit of a Christmas market, these markets are a true reflection of Norway's rich heritage and community spirit.

Unique Norwegian Handicrafts

Norwegian handicrafts reflect the country's rich cultural heritage, deep connection to nature, and centuries-old traditions. These handcrafted items are not only functional but also serve as beautiful expressions of Norwegian artistry and craftsmanship. Let's explore some of the most unique Norwegian handicrafts, enriched with personal experiences and observations.

1. Bunad Embroidery

Description:

• The bunad is a traditional Norwegian costume, often worn during special occasions and celebrations. Each region in Norway has its own distinct style of bunad, featuring intricate embroidery, patterns, and colors. The embroidery on a bunad is a true testament to the skill and artistry of Norwegian craftspeople.

Materials and Techniques:
• The embroidery on a bunad is typically done using high-quality wool or silk threads on woolen or linen fabric. Traditional motifs include flowers, leaves, and geometric patterns, often inspired by nature and local folklore. The embroidery is usually done by hand, requiring great precision and attention to detail.

• I had the opportunity to visit a workshop where skilled artisans were creating bunads. Watching them meticulously stitch the intricate patterns onto the fabric was mesmerizing. The vibrant colors and detailed designs were truly impressive, and I gained a deep appreciation for the time and effort that goes into making each bunad. Wearing a bunad during Constitution Day celebrations, I felt a strong sense of connection to Norwegian culture and tradition.

2. Rosemaling

Description:
• Rosemaling is a traditional Norwegian decorative painting style characterized by its flowing floral and scroll patterns. It is often used to adorn wooden objects such as furniture, bowls, and storage trunks. Rosemaling has its roots in the 18th century

and varies by region, each with its own distinct style and color palette.

Materials and Techniques:
• Rosemaling is typically done on wood using oil-based or acrylic paints. The designs are painted freehand, with an emphasis on fluid brushstrokes and graceful curves. Common motifs include flowers, leaves, and vines, often arranged in symmetrical patterns.

• I visited a museum in Telemark, a region known for its distinctive style of rosemaling. The beautifully painted wooden objects on display were a feast for the eyes. I even had the chance to participate in a rosemaling workshop, where I learned basic brush techniques and created my own small piece of painted wood. The experience gave me a deeper appreciation for the skill and creativity involved in this traditional art form.

3. Knitting and Textile Arts

Description:
• Knitting and textile arts are deeply ingrained in Norwegian culture, with a long tradition of creating warm and functional garments such as sweaters, mittens, and socks. Norwegian knitting patterns often feature geometric designs and motifs inspired by nature, such as snowflakes, stars, and reindeer.

Materials and Techniques:
• Norwegian knitters typically use high-quality wool yarn, known for its warmth and durability. Traditional techniques include colorwork (stranded knitting) and intricate patterns such as the Selbu rose and the Setesdal design. Hand-knitted garments are highly valued for their craftsmanship and uniqueness.

• While exploring a small village in the Lofoten Islands, I visited a local shop specializing in hand-knitted garments. The shelves were filled with beautifully crafted sweaters, each with its own unique pattern and color scheme. I learned about the history of Norwegian knitting and even purchased a cozy sweater with a traditional design. Wearing it on chilly evenings, I felt a sense of warmth and connection to the artisans who created it.

4. Sami Handicrafts (Duodji)

Description:
• Duodji is the traditional handicraft of the Sami people, the indigenous inhabitants of northern Norway. Sami handicrafts encompass a wide range of items, including clothing, accessories, tools, and decorative objects. These items are often made from natural materials such as reindeer hide, bone, and wood.

Materials and Techniques:
• Sami craftspeople use traditional techniques passed down through generations. Common materials include reindeer leather, bone, antler, and wood. Techniques such as sewing, carving, and beadwork are used to create functional and decorative items. Typical products include gákti (traditional Sami clothing), belts, knives, and jewelry.

• Visiting a Sami craft fair in Karasjok was a fascinating experience. The stalls were filled with beautifully crafted items, each reflecting the unique heritage of the Sami people. I was particularly drawn to the intricately beaded jewelry and the finely carved wooden items. The artisans were eager to share stories about their work and the cultural significance of their creations. I purchased a beautifully beaded bracelet, which serves as a cherished reminder of the rich Sami traditions.

5. Woodworking and Stave Churches

Description:
• Woodworking is a traditional craft in Norway, with a long history of creating functional and decorative wooden items. One of the most iconic examples of Norwegian woodworking is the stave church, a type of medieval wooden church with a unique architectural style. These churches are characterized by their intricate wood carvings and steep, tiered roofs.

Materials and Techniques:
• Norwegian woodworkers use high-quality timber, often sourced from local forests. Traditional woodworking techniques include carving, joinery, and painting. In addition to stave churches, woodworkers create a variety of items such as furniture, utensils, and decorative objects.

• Visiting the Borgund Stave Church was a highlight of my trip to Norway. The church's intricate wood carvings and architectural details were awe-inspiring. Inside, I marveled at the craftsmanship and the sense of history that permeated the space. Exploring a nearby woodworking shop, I saw artisans creating beautifully carved wooden items, each reflecting the rich tradition of Norwegian woodworking.

6. Ceramics and Pottery

Description:
• Norwegian ceramics and pottery are known for their quality and craftsmanship. Traditional pottery often features simple, functional designs with subtle decorations inspired by nature. Modern Norwegian ceramics continue to evolve, blending traditional techniques with contemporary aesthetics.

Materials and Techniques:
• Norwegian potters use high-quality clay and glazes to create their works. Techniques include wheel-throwing, hand-building, and glazing. Traditional motifs such as flowers, leaves, and geometric patterns are often incorporated into the designs.

• Visiting a pottery studio in the town of Røros, I was captivated by the beautiful ceramics on display. The pieces ranged from traditional bowls and plates to contemporary vases and sculptures. I had the opportunity to try my hand at wheel-throwing, guided by a skilled potter. The experience gave me a new appreciation for the art and effort involved in creating each piece.

Unique Norwegian handicrafts reflect the country's rich cultural heritage, deep connection to nature, and centuries-old traditions. From the intricate embroidery of bunads and the flowing patterns of rosemaling to the warm and functional knitted garments and the finely crafted Sami duodji, each handicraft tells a story of artistry and cultural identity. Exploring these traditional crafts provides a deeper understanding of Norway's heritage and a meaningful connection to its people and their creative expressions.

Popular Souvenir Ideas

Bringing home a piece of Norway is a wonderful way to remember your travels and share a bit of Norwegian culture with friends and family. Here are some popular and unique Norwegian souvenir ideas, enriched with personal experiences and observations:

1. Bunad Accessories

Description:
• Bunad accessories, such as brooches (sølje), belts, and scarves, are intricately designed pieces that complement the traditional Norwegian costume, the bunad. These accessories are often made of silver or gold and feature detailed patterns and motifs.

Why It's Special:
• These accessories are a beautiful representation of Norwegian craftsmanship and cultural heritage. They make elegant and meaningful souvenirs, whether you wear them or display them as decorative items.

• During my visit to a bunad shop in Bergen, I was captivated by the intricate designs of the silver brooches. I purchased a small sølje brooch, which now holds a special place in my collection of travel mementos. The craftsmanship and cultural significance of the piece make it a cherished reminder of my time in Norway.

2. Rosemaling Decor

Description:
• Rosemaling is a traditional Norwegian decorative painting style characterized by flowing floral and scroll patterns. Items adorned with rosemaling include wooden plates, bowls, and furniture.

Why It's Special:
• Rosemaling items are not only functional but also beautifully decorative. Each piece is a work of art, reflecting the skill and creativity of the artisan.

• I bought a small wooden plate decorated with rosemaling from a local market in Telemark. The vibrant colors and intricate patterns make it a standout piece in my home. It serves as a lovely reminder of the rich artistic traditions of Norway.

3. Norwegian Knitwear

Description:
• Norwegian knitwear, such as sweaters, mittens, and socks, is known for its warmth, quality, and distinctive patterns. Common motifs include the Selbu rose and the Setesdal design.

Why It's Special:
• Hand-knitted garments are both practical and stylish. They make perfect gifts for loved ones or a cozy addition to your own wardrobe.

• I couldn't resist purchasing a traditional Norwegian sweater from a shop in the Lofoten Islands. The intricate pattern and soft wool make it incredibly comfortable and warm. Wearing it brings back fond memories of the chilly evenings spent exploring the beautiful fjords.

4. Sami Handicrafts

Description:
• Sami handicrafts (duodji) include items such as gákti (traditional clothing), reindeer leather accessories, knives, and jewelry. These handcrafted items are often made using natural materials like reindeer hide, bone, and wood.

Why It's Special:
• Sami handicrafts are unique and reflect the rich cultural heritage of the indigenous Sami people. They make meaningful and culturally significant souvenirs.

• I visited a Sami craft fair in Karasjok and was drawn to the beautifully beaded jewelry. I bought a beaded bracelet, which is not only a stunning piece of craftsmanship but also a reminder of the warm hospitality and vibrant culture of the Sami people.

5. Norwegian Chocolates and Sweets

Description:
• Norway is known for its delicious chocolates and sweets. Popular brands include Freia and Nidar, offering a variety of chocolates, licorice, and other treats.

Why It's Special:
• Norwegian chocolates and sweets make delightful gifts and are perfect for sharing the flavors of Norway with friends and family.

• I stocked up on Freia chocolates and Nidar's lakris (licorice) during my visit to Oslo. These treats were a hit with my friends back home, and they enjoyed experiencing a taste of Norway.

6. Viking Souvenirs

Description:
• Viking-themed souvenirs, such as replica Viking ships, jewelry, and helmets, are popular mementos. These items often feature traditional Norse designs and symbols.

Why It's Special:
• Viking souvenirs are a fun and educational way to remember Norway's rich Viking heritage. They make great decorative items and conversation starters.

• I purchased a small replica Viking ship from the Viking Ship Museum in Oslo. The detailed craftsmanship and historical significance of the piece make it a cherished keepsake.

7. Norwegian Cookbooks and Recipes

Description:
• Cookbooks featuring traditional Norwegian recipes are a wonderful way to bring the flavors of Norway into your kitchen. These books often include recipes for dishes such as klippfisk (dried cod), kjøttkaker (meatballs), and traditional baked goods.

Why It's Special:
• A Norwegian cookbook allows you to recreate the delicious dishes you enjoyed during your travels and share them with friends and family.

• I bought a Norwegian cookbook from a local bookstore in Trondheim. The recipes have allowed me to recreate some of my favorite Norwegian dishes, and cooking them brings back fond memories of my culinary adventures in Norway.

8. Handmade Ceramics

Description:

• Handmade ceramics, such as bowls, mugs, and plates, are popular souvenirs. Norwegian ceramics often feature simple yet elegant designs inspired by nature.

Why It's Special:

• These handcrafted items are both functional and beautiful. They make excellent gifts and add a touch of Scandinavian design to your home.

• I purchased a set of handmade ceramic mugs from a pottery studio in Røros. The simple, earthy design and high-quality craftsmanship make them a joy to use. Each time I enjoy a warm drink, I'm reminded of the charming village and the talented artisans I met there.

Bringing home a piece of Norway through unique and meaningful souvenirs allows you to cherish the memories of your travels and share the beauty of Norwegian culture with others. Whether it's a beautifully embroidered bunad accessory, a cozy hand-knitted sweater, or a delicious bar of Freia chocolate, each souvenir tells a story and captures the essence of Norway's rich heritage.

Chapter 10. Safety and Practical Information

Emergency Contacts and Health Services

Here are the key emergency numbers you should know when in Norway:

• Police: 112
• Medical (Ambulance): 113
• Fire: 110
• Maritime & Mountain Rescue: 120
• Poison Information: +47 22 59 13 00
• Roadside Assistance: 02222

Health Services in Norway

Norway offers a comprehensive healthcare system. Here are some important contacts and services:

• **Helsenorge**: This is the national online health service portal where you can find information about your healthcare rights, schedule appointments, and access your medical records.
• **General Practitioner (GP):** Your GP is your most important contact for non-emergency medical issues. They can provide referrals to specialists and coordinate your care.
• **Out-of-hours Medical Service**: For urgent but non-life-threatening medical issues, you can contact the out-of-hours medical service by calling 116 117.
• **Specialist Healthcare**: For treatment by a specialist, you will need a referral from your GP. You can find information about hospitals and specialists through Helsenorge.

• **Emergency Health Care**: In case of a medical emergency, dial 113 to get immediate assistance.

Safety Precautions for Outdoor Activities

Exploring the natural beauty of Norway's fjords, mountains, and forests can be a thrilling experience, but it's important to take safety precautions to ensure a safe and enjoyable adventure. Here are some key safety tips for various outdoor activities:

General Outdoor Safety

1. Check Weather Conditions: Always check the weather forecast before heading out. Norwegian weather can be unpredictable, so be prepared for sudden changes and dress accordingly.

2. Plan Your Route: Research and plan your route in advance. Inform someone of your plans, including your expected return time. Carry a map, compass, and GPS device to navigate.

3. Dress in Layers: Wear moisture-wicking base layers, insulating mid-layers, and waterproof outer layers. Proper clothing will keep you warm, dry, and comfortable in varying conditions.

4. Stay Hydrated and Nourished: Bring enough water and high-energy snacks to keep you hydrated and fueled during your activity. Dehydration and lack of energy can affect your performance and safety.

5. Carry a First Aid Kit: Pack a basic first aid kit with essentials such as bandages, antiseptic wipes, pain relievers, and any personal medications. Be prepared to handle minor injuries and ailments.

6. Respect Nature and Wildlife: Follow the Leave No Trace principles by minimizing your impact on the environment. Stay on marked trails, pack out all trash, and avoid disturbing wildlife.

Hiking and Trekking Safety

1. Choose the Right Trail: Select a trail that matches your fitness level and experience. Start with easier trails if you're a beginner and gradually progress to more challenging routes.

2. Wear Proper Footwear: Invest in sturdy hiking boots with good ankle support and traction. Comfortable and well-fitted footwear is essential for preventing blisters and injuries.

3. Use Trekking Poles: Trekking poles can provide stability and reduce strain on your knees, especially during steep ascents and descents.

4. Stay on Marked Trails: Follow marked trails and avoid taking shortcuts. Straying from designated paths can lead to accidents and getting lost.

5. Monitor Your Energy Levels: Take regular breaks to rest and recharge. Listen to your body and avoid pushing yourself beyond your limits.

Kayaking and Paddleboarding Safety

1. Wear a Life Jacket: Always wear a properly fitted life jacket when kayaking or paddleboarding. It's a crucial safety measure that can save your life in case of an accident.

2. Check Water Conditions: Be aware of water conditions, including currents, tides, and wind. Avoid kayaking or paddleboarding in rough waters or strong winds.

3. Paddle with a Buddy: It's safer to paddle with a partner or in a group. If you're kayaking or paddleboarding alone, inform someone of your plans and expected return time.

4. Stay Close to Shore: When paddling in unfamiliar waters, stay close to the shore to reduce the risk of getting lost or encountering dangerous conditions.

5. Carry Safety Equipment: Bring essential safety equipment, such as a whistle, waterproof flashlight, and a dry bag for your valuables.

Glacier Exploration and Ice Climbing Safety

1. Join a Guided Tour: Glacier exploration and ice climbing require specialized skills and knowledge. Always join a guided tour led by experienced guides who can provide safety training and equipment.

2. Use Proper Gear: Wear crampons, ice axes, helmets, and other necessary gear for glacier travel and ice climbing. Ensure that your equipment is in good condition and fits properly.

3. Learn Basic Skills: Familiarize yourself with basic glacier travel and ice climbing techniques, including how to use crampons and ice axes, and how to self-arrest in case of a fall.

4. Be Aware of Crevasses: Glaciers are dynamic environments with hidden crevasses. Always follow your guide's instructions and stay on marked routes to avoid falling into crevasses.

5. Monitor Weather and Ice Conditions: Glacier conditions can change rapidly due to weather and temperature fluctuations. Stay informed about current conditions and be prepared to adjust your plans if necessary.

By taking these safety precautions, you can ensure a safe and enjoyable outdoor adventure in Norway. Whether you're hiking through scenic trails, paddling in pristine waters, or exploring majestic glaciers, being prepared and mindful of safety measures will enhance your experience and help you make the most of your time in Norway's beautiful natural landscapes.

Navigating Public Transportation

Navigating public transportation can be both an adventure and a necessity, especially when you're exploring new cities or traveling for work or leisure. Mastering the art of public transit can save you time, money, and stress, allowing you to experience a destination like a local. Here, we'll delve into the essentials of navigating public transportation, enriched with personal experiences and observations to make your journey smoother and more enjoyable.

1. Planning Your Journey

Use Technology to Your Advantage:
- Apps and Websites: Leverage transportation apps like Google Maps, Citymapper, or local transit apps to plan your route. These tools provide real-time updates, schedules, and alternate routes in case of delays.
- Online Timetables: Check the official websites of public transportation services for the latest schedules and route maps. Some cities also offer downloadable PDFs or interactive maps.

Understand the System:
- Routes and Lines: Familiarize yourself with the main routes and lines of buses, trams, trains, and subways. Knowing the major stops and transfer points can help you navigate more efficiently.
- Fare Zones: Be aware of fare zones, especially in large cities where the cost may vary depending on the distance traveled. Purchase the appropriate ticket or pass for your journey.

- During a trip to Paris, I found the Paris Metro app incredibly useful. It not only provided detailed maps and schedules but also had an offline mode, which was a lifesaver when I had no internet access.

2. Purchasing and Validating Tickets

Types of Tickets:
- Single Tickets: Suitable for one-time journeys. These can usually be purchased at ticket machines or kiosks at stations.
- Day Passes: Ideal for tourists, offering unlimited travel within a certain timeframe (e.g., 24 hours). They can save money if you plan to make multiple trips in a day.
- Season Tickets: For long-term stays, consider purchasing weekly or monthly passes for cost savings.

Where to Buy:
- Ticket Machines: Most stations have ticket machines that accept cash and cards. These machines often have language options for international travelers.
- Mobile Apps: Many cities offer mobile ticketing apps, allowing you to buy and store tickets on your smartphone. This can be more convenient and sometimes offers discounts.
- Retail Outlets: Some tickets can be purchased at convenience stores, newsstands, or authorized retailers.

Validating Tickets:
- Validation Machines: Ensure you validate your ticket before boarding. Look for validation machines at station entrances or on the vehicles themselves.

- Inspection: Keep your validated ticket accessible, as inspectors may ask to see it during your journey.

- In Rome, I learned the hard way about the importance of validating tickets. After boarding a bus without validating my ticket, I was fined by an inspector. Since then, I've always made sure to validate my tickets before starting my journey.

3. Boarding and Riding Public Transport

Boarding Etiquette:
- Queueing: In many cities, it's customary to form a queue while waiting for buses or trains. Respect the order and allow others to disembark before boarding.
- Priority Seating: Be mindful of seats designated for the elderly, disabled, or pregnant passengers. Offer your seat if someone in need boards the vehicle.

Navigating Crowded Conditions:
- Peak Hours: Avoid traveling during peak hours if possible, as vehicles can be crowded and less comfortable.
- Personal Space: In crowded conditions, be considerate of others' personal space. Keep bags and belongings close to you.

Safety and Comfort:
- Hold On: Always hold onto handrails or poles when the vehicle is in motion to avoid falls or injuries.
- Exit Strategy: Know your stop and prepare to disembark a few moments before arrival. Move towards the exit doors in advance.

- While traveling in Tokyo, I marveled at the efficiency and politeness of the commuters. Despite the crowded trains, everyone was respectful and orderly, making the experience much more pleasant.

4. Transfers and Connections

Planning Transfers:
- Transfer Points: Identify key transfer points on your route. These are major stations where you can switch between lines or modes of transport.
- Timeliness: Allow extra time for transfers, especially during busy periods or when traveling with luggage or children.

Using Interchange Stations:
- Signage: Follow clear signage at interchange stations. Symbols and colors often indicate different lines and directions.
- Information Desks: Don't hesitate to ask for help at information desks or from station staff if you're unsure about your transfer.

- In London, the comprehensive signage in the Underground made transferring between lines straightforward. The "mind the gap" announcements were a constant reminder to be cautious while boarding and alighting.

5. Emergency Situations

Stay Calm:
- Remain Composed: In case of an emergency, remain calm and follow the instructions of the transit staff. Panic can worsen the situation.
- Exit Routes: Familiarize yourself with emergency exits and safety procedures posted in the vehicle or station.

Seek Assistance:
- Help Points: Look for emergency help points or intercoms to communicate with staff in case of an issue.
- Medical Emergencies: If you or someone else requires medical assistance, inform the staff immediately and provide clear information about the situation.

- Once in Munich, I encountered a sudden train delay due to a technical issue. The staff kept passengers well-informed, and their calm demeanor helped everyone stay composed until the situation was resolved.

Navigating public transportation can greatly enhance your travel experience, offering an affordable, efficient, and immersive way to explore new places. With these tips, you can confidently traverse any public transport system, making the most of your journey.

I hope these extensive tips help you navigate public transportation with ease and confidence.

Essential Tips for Navigating Public Transport

Navigating public transport can be a breeze when you have the right tips. Whether you're in a bustling city or exploring the scenic countryside, these essential tips will help you make the most of your journey:

1. Plan Your Route
- Use Maps and Apps: Utilize apps like Google Maps or local transportation apps to plan your journey. They provide real-time

information on routes, schedules, and any delays.

- Check Schedules: Always check the timetables and schedules in advance to avoid long waits. Note that some routes may have different schedules on weekends or holidays.

2. Buy Tickets in Advance

- Online and Mobile Tickets: Purchase tickets online or through mobile apps to save time. Many cities offer discounted fares for advance purchases.
- Ticket Machines: Familiarize yourself with ticket machines at stations. They are usually user-friendly and have multiple language options.
- Correct Fare: Make sure you have the correct fare for your journey. Some buses and trams may not provide change.

3. Validate Your Ticket

- Ticket Validation: Ensure you validate your ticket before boarding, especially for trains, trams, and buses. Look for validation machines at stations or on vehicles.
- Keep Your Ticket: Retain your ticket until the end of your journey, as you may need to show it during inspections.

4. Know Your Stops and Transfers

- Identify Stops: Know the names of the stops where you need to board and alight. Write them down or save them on your phone.
- Transfers: If your journey involves transfers, note the connecting routes and stops. Allow extra time for transfers, especially in large stations.

5. Be Punctual

- Arrive Early: Arrive at your stop or station a few minutes early. Public transport can be punctual, and missing a bus or train can lead to delays.
- Boarding: Allow passengers to disembark before boarding. Stand clear of the doors and wait for your turn.

6. Safety and Etiquette

- Stay Alert: Be aware of your surroundings, especially in crowded areas or during late-night travel. Keep your belongings secure and close to you.
- Respect Local Customs: Follow local customs and etiquette, such as giving up your seat to elderly or disabled passengers.
- Personal Space: Be mindful of personal space and avoid blocking aisles or doors.

7. Accessibility

- Assistive Services: If you have mobility issues, check for assistive services such as ramps, elevators, and priority seating.
- Announcements: Pay attention to announcements for any changes in service or important information.

8. Emergency Information

- Emergency Exits: Familiarize yourself with the location of emergency exits and safety procedures on the vehicle.
- Emergency Contacts: Keep a list of emergency contacts and relevant information with you at all times.

9. Language Tips

- Basic Phrases: Learn a few basic phrases in the local language, such as asking for directions or help. This can be incredibly useful when navigating public transport.

10. Enjoy the Journey
- Scenic Routes: Take advantage of scenic routes and enjoy the views. Public transport often offers unique perspectives of the local landscape.
- Relax and Explore: Use the time to relax, read a book, or plan your next destination. Enjoy the journey as much as the destination.

By following these essential tips, you'll find navigating public transport to be a smooth and enjoyable experience. Whether you're commuting in a bustling city or exploring new places, these tips will help you make the most of your travels.

Safety Tips

General Safety Tips
1. Follow Ship Rules: Always adhere to the cruise line's safety guidelines and instructions from the crew.
2. Life Jacket: Familiarize yourself with the location of life jackets and participate in the mandatory safety drill.
3. Stay Informed: Keep an eye on the ship's daily schedule and announcements for any updates or changes.
4. Emergency Exits: Know the location of emergency exits and stairways on the ship.
5. Health Precautions: Wash your hands frequently and use hand sanitizer, especially before meals.

Onboard Safety
1. Balcony Safety: Keep balcony doors locked when not in use and supervise children closely.
2. Staircase Safety: Hold onto handrails when using stairs and avoid running.
3. Deck Safety: Be cautious when walking on the deck, especially during rough seas. Avoid leaning over railings.
4. Alcohol Consumption: Drink responsibly and be aware of your limits to avoid accidents or injuries.

Excursion Safety
1. Listen to Guides: Pay attention to the instructions given by excursion guides and follow their directions.
2. Stay with the Group: Always stay with your group during excursions and avoid wandering off on your own.
3. Weather Awareness: Check the weather forecast before heading out and dress appropriately for the conditions.
4. Hydration: Stay hydrated, especially during outdoor activities, and carry a water bottle with you.

Health and Wellness
1. Motion Sickness: If you're prone to seasickness, consider taking medication and choose a cabin in the middle of the ship on a lower deck for added stability.
2. First Aid: Familiarize yourself with the location of first aid stations and carry any necessary medications with you.
3. Sun Protection: Use sunscreen, wear a hat, and stay hydrated to protect yourself from sunburn and heat exhaustion.
4. Medical Conditions: Inform the cruise staff about any medical conditions or special needs you may have.

Personal Safety
1. Secure Belongings: Keep your valuables in a safe or locked cabin and use the ship's safe deposit boxes if available.

2. Be Cautious: Be aware of your surroundings and avoid sharing personal information with strangers.

3. Travel Insurance: Ensure you have travel insurance that covers medical emergencies and trip cancellations.

4. Emergency Contacts: Keep a list of emergency contacts and important information with you at all times.

Environmental Awareness

1. Respect Nature: Follow guidelines for wildlife encounters and avoid disturbing natural habitats.

2. Reduce Waste: Minimize your environmental impact by recycling and disposing of waste properly.

3. Stay Clean: Use designated areas for swimming and avoid polluting the water.

By following these safety tips, you can enjoy your Norwegian fjord cruise with peace of mind. Have an amazing adventure and take in all the breathtaking scenery and experiences the fjords have to offer!

Chapter 11. Sample Itineraries

One-Day Excursions

1. Ålesund from Fjords to Trolls: Explore the beautiful town of Ålesund with its stunning fjords and unique troll sculptures. Duration: 7.5 hours.

2. Bergen Ultimate Sightseeing Tour: Discover the highlights of Bergen, including the UNESCO-listed Bryggen wharf and the historic Bergenhus Fortress. Duration: 4 hours.

3. Geiranger Shore Excursion: Enjoy breathtaking views of the Geirangerfjord, including a visit to the Eagle Road and Mount Dalsnibba. Duration: 3-4 hours.

Weekend Getaways

1. Oslo City Break: Experience the vibrant capital city with its museums, galleries, and charming neighborhoods. Enjoy a Sunday stroll through the city's parks and gardens.

2. Tromsø Northern Lights Chase: Visit Tromsø, the gateway to the Arctic, and join a small group Northern Lights chase. Duration: 3-4 days.

3. Arctic Island Retreat: Spend a weekend on the beautiful Manshausen island, surrounded by mountains and sea. Enjoy activities like kayaking and relaxing in your seacabin.

Extended Stays

1. Scandic Victoria Oslo: Stay in the heart of Oslo with access to a gym, sauna, and traditional Norwegian cuisine at the Bristol Grill.

2. Hotel Bristol: Located in Oslo, this elegant hotel offers free Wi-Fi, gym, and sauna access, along with live piano music at the Library Bar.

3. Norway in a Nutshell: Experience the classic Norwegian fjord tour with scenic train rides and fjord cruises. Duration: 1 day or more.

One-Week Itinerary for Norway

Embark on an unforgettable journey through Norway, exploring its stunning landscapes, vibrant cities, and rich cultural heritage. This one-week itinerary covers the best of Norway, from the bustling capital of Oslo to the breathtaking fjords and charming coastal towns.

Day 1: Arrive in Oslo

Morning:
• Arrive in Oslo, Norway's capital city.
• Check into your hotel and freshen up.

Afternoon:
• Explore the Vigeland Sculpture Park, featuring over 200 sculptures by Gustav Vigeland.
• Visit the Royal Palace and stroll through the Palace Park.

Evening:
• Enjoy a leisurely dinner at a local restaurant and sample traditional Norwegian cuisine.
• Take a evening walk along the Aker Brygge waterfront.

Day 2: Oslo Sightseeing

Morning:
• Visit the Viking Ship Museum to see well-preserved Viking ships and artifacts.
• Explore the Norwegian Folk Museum to learn about traditional Norwegian culture and architecture.

Afternoon:
• Discover the National Museum, home to famous works such as Edvard Munch's "The Scream."
• Take a guided tour of the Akershus Fortress, a medieval castle with stunning views of the Oslofjord.

Evening:
• Enjoy a dinner cruise on the Oslofjord, taking in the beautiful scenery as you dine.

Day 3: Travel to Bergen

Morning:
• Take a scenic train ride from Oslo to Bergen on the Bergen Line. The journey offers breathtaking views of the Norwegian countryside.

Afternoon:
• Arrive in Bergen and check into your hotel.
• Explore the historic Bryggen wharf, a UNESCO World Heritage site with colorful wooden buildings.

Evening:
• Ride the Fløibanen funicular to the top of Mount Fløyen for panoramic views of Bergen.
• Dine at a seafood restaurant in the city center, savoring fresh catches from the nearby waters.

Day 4: Bergen and Surroundings

Morning:
• Visit the Hanseatic Museum to learn about Bergen's history as a major trading center.
• Explore the Bergenhus Fortress and its historic buildings.

Afternoon:
• Take a fjord cruise to the nearby Hardangerfjord, known for its stunning landscapes and fruit orchards.
• Visit the Steinsdalsfossen waterfall, where you can walk behind the cascading water.

Evening:
• Return to Bergen and enjoy dinner at a local restaurant.

Day 5: Travel to Flåm and Nærøyfjord

Morning:
• Take a train from Bergen to Flåm, a picturesque village nestled in the Aurlandsfjord.
• Check into your hotel in Flåm.

Afternoon:
• Embark on a fjord cruise through the Nærøyfjord, one of the narrowest and most beautiful fjords in Norway.
• Visit the Undredal Stave Church, one of Norway's smallest stave churches.

Evening:
• Enjoy a cozy dinner at a local inn in Flåm, sampling regional specialties.

Day 6: Flåm and Stegastein Viewpoint

Morning:
• Take a ride on the Flåm Railway, one of the world's most scenic train journeys, with breathtaking views of mountains and waterfalls.
• Visit the Flåm Railway Museum to learn about the history of this engineering marvel.

Afternoon:
• Drive or take a bus to the Stegastein Viewpoint, offering spectacular panoramic views of the Aurlandsfjord.

Evening:
• Return to Flåm and enjoy a relaxing evening at your hotel.

Day 7: Travel Back to Oslo

Morning:
• Depart Flåm and take the train back to Oslo, enjoying the scenic journey once again.

Afternoon:
• Arrive in Oslo and spend your last day exploring any remaining attractions or shopping for souvenirs.

Evening:
• Enjoy a farewell dinner at a fine dining restaurant in Oslo, reflecting on your memorable journey through Norway.

Made in the USA
Monee, IL
21 March 2025

14370211R00046

This one-week itinerary offers a perfect blend of Norway's natural beauty, cultural heritage, and vibrant cities. From the bustling streets of Oslo to the serene fjords and charming coastal towns, each day is filled with unforgettable experiences and breathtaking views.